Numenéra

THE GLIMMERING VALLEY

CREDITS

Designer	Monte Cook
Creative Director	Monte Cook
Developer	Shanna Germain
Managing Editor	Teri Litorco
Editor	Megan Boatright
Proofreader	Ray Vallese
Art Director	Bear Weiter
Layout Design	Javier P. Beltrán
Layout Assistance	Hannah Baker
Cover Artist	Russell Marks
Cartographer	Hugo Solis

Artists

Giuseppe De iure, Gaia Degl'Innocenti, Joel Chaim Holtzman,
Anton Kagounkin Magdalina, Guido Kuip, Macli, Russell Marks,
Andrea Negroponte, Mirco Paganessi, Grzegorz Pedrycz,
Bruno Senigalha, Lie Setiawan, Jessé Suursoo, Ben Wootten

Playtesters

Bruce R. Cordell, Dominique Dickey, Kate Evans,
Sean K. Reynolds, Teri Litorco

Monte Cook Games™

TABLE OF CONTENTS

INTRODUCTION

A free PDF version of the Player's Guide is available at: mymcg.info/tgv-pg

The Glimmering Valley is lush and fertile, belying the fact that, aeons earlier, it likely served as the site of an ancient complex or perhaps even a city. The people there are deliberately, almost fervently, simple in both life and outlook. But the Ninth World rejects simplicity, as nature abhors a vacuum.

The village of Neandran lies so deep in the valley that most people don't even know it exists. Even though it is built around an ancient structure between two crystalline monoliths, Neandran is a simple place, its folk having no contact with the world beyond the valley and little knowledge of the prior worlds and the wonders of the numenera. One might be tempted to say that Neandran is perhaps one of the most mundane spots in the Ninth World.

Except, of course, for the dream.

Everyone has the dream, each and every night upon falling into slumber. It's the only dream they have ever experienced. The dream is both alien and familiar. Alien because it shows people, things, and vistas not only unknown, but indeed impossible. Familiar because it is always the same, and always has been the same, since anyone has lived in the valley. Every odd color and unorthodox shape is as detailed in memory as one's home and the trees and grass just outside the door. Every unwonted creature and their inexplicable activities are as immediate and true as one's own human family. The folk of the valley have adopted words to speak of some of what they all dream, but these words have no value in describing any aspect of the waking world, for those colors, shapes, vistas, and creatures do not exist there. Despite its intimate relationship with the psyche of everyone in the village, the dream's complete disassociation from anything known or understood is enough to keep it forever unsettling.

For some, the dream does not come only at night. It can be experienced as a vision while one is awake, particularly if the person is in a relaxed state. Those who have these visions describe it as "opening one's mind to allow the dream to come in," but few do so intentionally. Some say the ability to intersect the dream as a waking vision depends on where you are and what time of day it is. In all the generations, however, not even the wise folk have ascertained the rules of how it all works—if there are rules at all.

Everyone in Neandran knows this is how it is. How it's always been. How it always will be. This is the dream that their parents had, and their grandparents before them.

And then, less than two weeks ago, the dream changed.

Numenera Discovery | **Numenera Destiny**

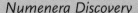

Throughout this book, you'll see page references to various items accompanied by these two symbols. These are page references to *Numenera Discovery* and *Numenera Destiny*, respectively, where you can find additional details about that rule, ability, creature, or concept. Often, it will be necessary to look up the reference to find information you need. Other times, it's not necessary, but looking it up can deepen your experience and understanding of the setting.

A CAMPAIGN STARTER

The Glimmering Valley is designed to provide everything you need to start a Numenera campaign and carry it through for many game sessions. It provides player characters an origin point, a home to defend, and support characters to fill out their background. It presents an overarching mystery with plenty of paths to take, places to explore, challenges to overcome, and discoveries to make. It introduces the concepts of Numenera over time, so that new players can acclimate themselves to the setting through their actions, all the while presenting new concepts for experienced players.

As of this writing, Numenera is ten years old. Over that decade, we've published a variety of books and taken the game to a variety of locations, from the ocean depths to the far reaches of space—even to other dimensions. We've designed adventures and sourcebooks that present different play styles, including epics that take characters across the map and well beyond.

But some people—particularly those new to the game or those thinking about starting a new campaign—have looked at all these books and said, "This is all really cool, but where do I start?" Others have asked, "I'm excited to eventually have the PCs travel to the *Edge of the Sun* and into the *Voices of the Datasphere* but how do I get things going initially?" In other words, with all the possibilities the game and the setting offer, it can seem at first like there are *too many* options. I'm sympathetic to that point of view. I love all of our Numenera products, but I'm also interested in taking things back to their roots.

To me, "the roots" are characters from humble beginnings who not only don't know about the huge world that lies outside their door, they don't even know what's on the other side of the river that runs near their home. The science of the prior worlds is little more than tales of ancient magic to them. Most of the animals and creatures that prowl the lonely stretches of their world are nigh-unimaginable monsters and demons. Ruins of past civilizations are the haunted domains of sorcery and devilish spirits. The characters themselves might have powers and abilities that they don't truly understand.

In other words, it's about the unknown. Although *Numenera* comes with a gorgeous poster map filled with kingdoms and mountains and deserts and strangely named places, in reality the game—at its core—wasn't originally designed with the idea of showing that map to the players and explaining the truths of the larger world. Imagine you're playing a video game and instead of a big world map, it starts with your location as a little dot in the middle of an otherwise black screen. You can zoom out all you want, but it's all just unknown darkness until you actually go and investigate yourself. The map locations don't manifest until you discover them.

That, to me, is the beginning of a Numenera game. Maybe in the later stages of a campaign you're dealing with the rulers of Thaemor, or sailing across the sea, or negotiating peace with Gaians, but to start with, all you know is that the world is a big, mysterious, and frankly frightening place. Leaving your home and venturing into the wilderness beyond your ken takes real courage. And to survive out there takes real skill.

So that's what *The Glimmering Valley* is all about. The PCs start in a little village that, while it has its own strangeness, is relatively safe but also decidedly isolated. Sure, a few people that live there can tell tales of the strange beasts in the woods, the bandits that prey on those traveling the paths, and even the Old Witch that lives in a magic house, but for the most part, the only way to learn about the valley (and the world) the PCs live in is to go explore it. (And in so doing, discover that some of those beasts, those bandits, and even the Old Witch are not at all what they initially seemed.)

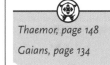

Thaemor, page 148

Gaians, page 134

FOR THE GM

R unning *The Glimmering Valley* is no
more or less difficult than any other
Numenera adventure content, but it's
absolutely worth it to read through the
material to get the right understanding
so that you can portray the setting, the
non-player characters (NPCs), and the
events in the way that is best for the players.

You don't need to read this entire book to
start running the game, however.

Familiarize yourself with this chapter and
the next one on creating characters. Get to
really know the Neandran chapter. And then
read through the locations in The Valley that
are near Neandran.

STEP BY STEP

First of all, recognize that you shouldn't
hand your players both *Numenera Discovery*
and *Destiny* (or even the original *Numenera*
corebook) and say, "Anything goes."
Character options are more limited for
characters starting in this setting, although
there are still many to choose from. Take a
look at the next chapter and you'll see that
only Glaive, Nano, and Jack characters are
available at the start. Foci are limited to
those that don't require a lot of background
with or exposure to ancient devices,
because in Neandran, such things truly are
not very common.

Your group can spend the entire first
session just interacting with the NPCs that
live in Neandran, so having a good idea of
who they are, what they're like, and what
they might have to offer or say is important.
You can also start things off with the group
headed out of town to do some exploring. It
really depends on what the group as a whole
will find most interesting and entertaining.

More than anything, however, the
direction in which the player characters
(PCs) first head off (whenever they do)
should be up to them. With the information
provided in the Player's Guide, they know of
the lake and the oracle, the bandits, and the
old witch. There's also the dream that has
recently changed that might prompt further
exploration of the valley—or the PCs might
just want to head off into the woods to see
what they can see.

The point is, they should choose where
to go from these options. You want to let
them know right at the start that you're
not leading them by the nose somewhere.
There's no one in Neandran that can really
tell them what to do or where to go.

Some people use the term "sandbox
game" to describe this sort of campaign,
with the idea being that the GM presents
a sandbox to play in, and the players can
choose to go and do whatever they want.
The Glimmering Valley isn't a sandbox game
to a purist, most likely, but the general
concept is there.

The PCs can go where they want, so the
GM needs to be ready when they do. There
are plenty of nearby locations to explore
as well as challenges in the form of local
fauna (and some of the flora) and the
valley encounters that can happen as the
PCs explore. These, of course, can lead the
PCs to some of the locations detailed in
Chapter 4: The Valley.

And *The Glimmering Valley* isn't just
about location-based adventures. There
are event-based scenarios that occur as
time goes on—first and foremost the
construction of the Uldada that disrupts
Neandran life significantly.

Player's Guide, page 120
Lake Memory, page 36
Oracle, page 36
Bandits, page 37
Old Witch, page 39
The dream, page 10

Creating Characters
for the Glimmering
Valley, page 14

Chapter 3: Neandran,
page 22

Chapter 4: The Valley,
page 32

GM is the short for
game master.

Valley Encounters,
page 44

Uldada, page 93
You can also use this
setting as more of a
sandbox if you don't
enforce the clock
on the Uldada.

THE MOOD AND TONE

The idea of *The Glimmering Valley* is that the PCs start out rather sheltered and ignorant. The entire mini-campaign is really about the loss of innocence and a coming of age—an awareness that there is a larger context, in terms both of the world and of time. It's about venturing into the unknown, and discovering just how amazing and dangerous the world can be.

PCs interested in wealth and power will find some shins, oddities, cyphers, and maybe even an artifact. But far more interesting, they'll develop skills and powers within themselves, and find a bit about the truth of their world.

The mood, then, is about huddling near the campfire in the dark of night, but eventually gathering the courage to explore that darkness. The wilderness might not be there to be tamed, but it can be survived by those who are smart and capable, and perhaps most important of all, the only way to survive—let alone prosper—long term is to discover at least a little of what lies beyond hearth and home. Numenera may be at least somewhat about isolation, but that doesn't mean that isolation is the goal. It might be about ignorance of the true nature of the world, but at least some of that ignorance can be overcome, and that's the goal of this campaign.

The product is very deliberately designed with this approach in mind. The characters start in a little isolated village, begin to explore it, learn a little about it, and then, at the other end of the valley, the world quite literally opens up before them.

IF THIS IS YOUR FIRST NUMENERA CAMPAIGN

An isolated village. Bandits causing trouble. Monsters in the woods. If these all sound like the starting positions of a standard fantasy roleplaying game (RPG), it's because they are. It's the intention of this setup to put players (at least those who have played other RPGs, or have read or watched fantasy fiction) in somewhat familiar territory.

The idea isn't to hit the players over the head with "It's science fantasy! Ancient technology! Everything is weird!" Rather, use the setup of the Glimmering Valley to ease them into it. Start with mystery and move toward weird.

By the time they get to Ketterach or they explore the Ancient Crèche, or the Uldada gets to its latter stages, things will be very science fantasy and very weird.

Let the players go and do what they wish, but don't encourage or even enable them to run out to the valley right away. Allow the Glimmering Valley to unfold before the PCs. Don't rush through anything. Don't accelerate character progression. If the players want to spend a whole session in Neandran, and another literally just poking around in the woods, let them. As long as everyone's having fun, it's all good.

USING THE GLIMMERING VALLEY IN AN EXISTING CAMPAIGN

You could have Numenera characters from elsewhere come into the valley and experience the events there, explore the Ancient Crèche and other locations, and so on.

My honest advice? Don't do it.

It's your game and you can do as you please, but this entire product has been designed with the idea that the PCs have lived their whole lives in the little village detailed here and begin to explore the valley in which it lies and perhaps, eventually, the world beyond.

In a lot of games, the PCs are outsiders who arrive in a location, find out the interesting thing going on or learn of the local problem, and deal with it. It's very much an Old West aesthetic with the PCs taking on the roles of the heroes wandering from town to town. In *The Glimmering Valley*, the core concept is "This is *our* valley. Our home." It really focuses on where the PCs are from and makes that not some vague backstory, but the actual story.

As outsiders, the PCs are likely to react to the situations differently, and certainly the NPCs would treat them differently. Plus, they'd almost certainly experience things in reverse order, arriving at the Glimmering Valley and reaching Ketterach first and Neandran last. That could still be interesting, but I think trying to use the material here as designed will give a very different and rewarding experience.

WEATHER AND TIME

Start the campaign in the middle of autumn. Folks in Neandran don't name the months—they number them, with the end of winter (which is the equivalent of March) being "Twelve" or "Twelvemonth." In the middle of autumn, the month is Sixthmonth.

Ideally, many of the current issues presented in this book can be wrapped up in about four months of game time (although this can and will vary from group to group). That means that, if the campaign starts in midfall, it will end as spring arrives.

Fall is, not surprisingly, the time when the days shorten, the leaves begin to turn color and fall to the forest floor, and the temperatures turn cool, but not yet cold.

Light rain falls frequently during winter months, and the sky remains grey and overcast for almost the entire season. Once winter begins, there's a chance for snow in the valley, but usually only a few inches at a time. It does get very cold, however, with both Loe's River and Lake Memory freezing over enough that they can be walked upon for at least a month in the middle of winter.

Lastly, thanks to the steep valley walls, the period of daylight seems shorter than it is outside of the valley. Dawn and dusk are both blocked by the sides of the valley, creating a much longer period of dim gloaming before the sun fully rises into sight, and after it has disappeared.

THE ADVENTURES AND STORIES IN THE VALLEY

The adventure content in this product comes in two forms: location-based and event-based content. GMs will want to utilize both at the same time, threading them together. Which means that sometimes event-based material might slightly change location-based material, at least in its significance. For example, when the PCs discover the Dterrase in the Ancient Crèche after they've determined they need it to cope with the Uldada, it will be more meaningful.

Location-Based: In chapters 3-8 on Neandran, the Valley, the Ancient Crèche, The Haunted Stair, and Ketterach, this book presents locations where adventures can take place. If the PCs literally just leave home and go exploring, they're likely to get involved in all sorts of exciting adventures.

Event-Based: The chapters about the briinii, the Uldada, the ourach invasion, and Essatha give information to use in event-based adventures. This material is keyed less to locations and more to time (or various triggers based on—usually—time). Events involving the Uldada happen early on, but the others get folded in later, so you have time to become familiar with all of them.

Dterrase, page 99

Uldada, page 93

Thanks to limited light in the valley and the density of the woods, people often use the "dark woods," the "shadowed wilderness," and similar references to describe the landscape of the forests. Natives long ago adapted to acting in dim light, and often time their daily routines around when actual daylight is available to complete tasks suited to the bright light.

Obviously, local flora and fauna are adapted to the daylight cycles and the weather conditions in the valley.

A billion years in the future, the distance of the moon suggests a 28-hour day, a 26-day-long lunar month, and a 312-day year.

Glimmer, page 43

Character Advancement, page 128

CHARACTER PROGRESSION

Progression through the tiers should be steady. The players should always feel the forward progression no matter what is going on in the story.

GMs should consider awarding enough XP so that all PCs gain one advancement step per session. Or perhaps three steps every four sessions, assuming those sessions are about four to five hours in length. This can be managed through GM intrusions as well as awards for discovery and accomplishment.

The Glimmering Valley likely holds enough to occupy (and hopefully captivate) characters to at least tier 3. This suggests a series of about twelve to fifteen game sessions, or to look at it another way, at least fifty hours of gameplay.

GMs, of course, could easily expand on material here based on the players' preferences and extend this to be a full campaign all the way to tier 6. Alternatively, some of the material here can be skipped over to make the campaign shorter, although unless the PCs literally just head out of the valley immediately and ignore most of what they see, expect them to spend at least four sessions there and attain tier 2 in or around Ketterach.

THE DREAM

The dream that everyone in Neandran experiences each night is a sort of glimmer. Beneath the village lies a device that is transmitting an ancient message, and while the intended receivers are aeons gone, the subconscious minds of humans have become attuned to it. But of course, they can't really make much sense out of it.

The GM shouldn't worry about describing the dream to players. In fact, the point is, it's impossible to describe the events in the dream because there are no words or context to do so—the dream involves colors, sounds, and images no human has ever experienced before. Instead, describe the *idea* of the dream. That is to say, images are utterly beyond the experience of the character. Unfamiliar shapes and colors. Strange sounds, including something that might be a language no one can decipher. Creatures, objects, and places no one has ever seen.

Describe the *feeling* of the dream. It's unsettlingly alien, and yet familiar in that the character experiences it each and every night. People have developed a few words for things seen in the dream, but the words have absolutely no use other than to describe what they dream.

- There's a color of the dream locals call *vell*.
- There's a creature locals call *the toothed eye*.
- There's a structure locals call *the growing forest of steel*.
- There's a sound locals call *the wailing of the wood*.

Newcomers to Neandran or the immediate area around the village who go to sleep also immediately begin having the dream. It's an unsettling experience, and the day after is one likely filled with anxiety and disorientation. In fact, it takes a week before most people are no longer adversely affected by each night's (identical) dream.

THE CHANGED DREAM

The dream changed about two weeks before the start of the campaign. The most dramatic part of the change is that some of the dream is slightly comprehensible. The vast majority of it is still alien, and many of the new inexplicable sights and sounds are different from those in the old dream—although some have remained, and a bit has just changed. For example, the creature that Neandrans have named the toothed eye is now smaller, while the growing forest of steel is taller and has a different orientation.

The comprehensible parts, however, show places in the valley that can be identified. The River Ring is glimpsed, for example, although the surrounding terrain appears less forested and the river is nowhere to be seen. The so-called toothed eye is seen floating through the trees, whereas before it had been inside some sort of structure. There's also an angular tower of metal and glass, but next to it is the same crystal-topped pole as stands near the Haunted Stair. Lastly, a section of the valley wall along the eastern side can be seen, although the cliffs appear to be even more regular in shape and not at all made of stone (but rather metal, glass, and synth). A large doorway here stands open. This latter site is in fact the Ancient Crèche, but it would take a lot of exploring to determine this.

More than anything, however, the big change is the sound referred to as the wailing of the wood. Rather than being a somewhat subtle (albeit disturbing) background noise as it always has been, now it grows louder and more intense as the dream goes on. There is little doubt to the dreamer that some impending event approaches, and it is very likely something dire.

THE MEANING OF THE DREAM

Who can fully understand the sights and sounds of the prior worlds? Certainly, those from Neandran cannot. However, it is worth noting that the dream—which is actually a transmission, remember—has to do with the events of the Uldada. But it is a transmission from a culture and a species utterly unlike ours or those of the Ninth World so it is not (to the PCs' minds) at all clear or straightforward. A few important

notes that can be gleaned in the course of the campaign include these:

- The Abrustraithe, the most important part of the Uldada, is *vell*-colored. This is notable to any Neandran that sees it.
- The toothed eye is actually a real (biomechanical) creature that currently hibernates in its lair in the valley, but it will come out to protect the Uldada. If the PCs see it, they will recognize it immediately.
- The growing forest of steel is the structure that begins to rise after the tremors end—the Uldada. Valley folk that see it will recognize it as such, and even though they've always thought they were seeing metal trees, they will now see they were dreaming of growing support beams originating from the ground and stretching horizontally as well to form a superstructure.
- The wailing of the wood is a sort of alarm that has to do with the timeline of the rising structure and its purpose (which is ultimately unknown and likely unknowable, but the important thing is, it indicates that the structure is coming). There is no literal wailing. The "alarm" is only in the dream. But it is communicating the inevitability of the Uldada.

DREAMING AWAY FROM THE VALLEY

It's important to note that people from Neandran have no concept of dreams other than the one they all share. Moving away from the valley will be disconcerting because the characters will begin to have normal subconscious-driven dreams, meaning that much of them will be about the dreamer's actual waking experiences.

Stranger still, because it's so ingrained in their minds (forevermore), they'll have the Glimmering Valley dream sometimes too. But now it will change, and become less precise and regular—in the way normal dreams do.

River Ring, page 41

Haunted Stair, page 50

Ancient Crèche, page 61

Uldada, page 93

For a list of major NPCs, creatures, places, devices, and concepts in the Glimmering Valley, you can refer to the Glossary and Index on page 128.

OTHER GLIMMERS

The GM should feel free to introduce other glimmers throughout the PCs' time in the valley. It is, after all, the name of the valley. Most of these should be just snippets from the dream, but occasionally (particularly farther away from Neandran) might involve other images or sounds. Like the dream, the glimmers should be mostly incomprehensible but occasionally might provide understandable—and perhaps even useful—information.

Creating Characters, page 14

Glimmers are a great way to give players a bit of a hint or a suggestion, but you shouldn't overuse them. Consider sometimes giving a glimmer to a PC that they don't really understand until they get to the right place or the right time.

Also consider having glimmers come to PCs when they are in a spot where they've experienced a previous glimmer, or at the same time of day. Allow the PCs to try to game this system, but doing so successfully should only work sporadically. (The data-transfer sequence is beyond Ninth World human understanding.)

WEIRD, MEANINGLESS GLIMMER EXAMPLES

- A garble of sounds that might be words, each accompanying a different color
- A vision of a series of cube shapes that seem to count to eleven (first there is one cube, then two, then three, and so on until eleven)
- A vision of an interior location where a bulbous, multi-headed creature squats on the wall as if it were the floor
- A sequence of sounds so complex that it could be music

MEANINGFUL GLIMMER EXAMPLES

- A vision wherein the character can just about make out the details of a map or schematic that shows their position and the position of the Ancient Crèche. It is brief, but if the PC acts on the knowledge relatively quickly, they can remember enough to get them fairly close.
- The sound of footsteps going down metal stairs. If tested, the sound of going down the Haunted Stair is identical.
- A vision of shapes and images that indicates how long before the next stage of the Uldada begins
- A vision of the ourach horde moving through the woods
- A vision of some of the important aspects of connecting the Dterrase to the Abrustraithe in the Uldada

INTRODUCING THE PLAYERS

The material in the Player's Guide should be given to the players, obviously. It provides an overview of what they would know as natives of Neandran. Most of the prominent figures and locations in the village are mentioned there, as well as general things they need to know regarding the valley, what lives there, and so on. The material from chapter 2 on creating characters is also distilled there, but you'll want to provide advice and information regarding character choices too.

A few things that players might be expecting are not present in the Glimmering Valley. A basic overview of some of those would include:

- Ironically, people don't use the word "numenera" much in Neandran. It's all just sorcery to them—even the Old Witch talks about magic, not science. In Ketterach, that's different. In general, Ketterach is more like a "standard" Numenera setting, if there is such a thing.
- Concepts like "the sea," "the desert," and so on are more akin to fairy tales than reality in the minds of everyone in Neandran and many in the rest of the valley.
- Shins don't mean much in Neandran. Everyone just gets what they need, more or less. (Ask for more than you need and Luttan, the villager in charge of the storehouses, will become cross.) Shins are talked about more than they are used. For example, if the PCs go to the Old Witch, she might refer to the value of her potions as being 10 shins, but she doesn't actually want shins. She wants the equivalent in something she can use. It's just a unit to facilitate bartering. Mostly, shins are used when trading with outsiders.
- The folk of Neandran might have heard the term "Aeon Priest" once or twice, but it's not something that they give any thought to. Both "Aeon Priests" and "the numenera" are Ketterach matters, and don't concern them. They don't know of the Order of Truth, nor do they refer to their language as "the Truth." They don't refer to it as anything, actually, and don't know any other languages to compare it to.

- None of the creatures in the rulebooks, other than seskii, are familiar to folks in the village. They don't know the terms abhuman, visitant, extraterrestrial, ultraterrestrial, or anything of the kind.
- People from Neandran have no concept of the Steadfast and the Beyond, or any of the lands or places beyond the valley.
- Players will almost certainly want a map of the valley, but there are none to be found in Neandran. Accurate cartography is a difficult skill unknown in the village, although most would be able to make a crude (and likely quite inaccurate) sketch of the layout of the area. It's difficult to always fully understand distances and direction while hiking through dense forest, so that makes an accurate map difficult to make and difficult to use. Instead, experienced travelers, like Mert, a hunter in Neandran, know step-by-step directions to get to important locations in the woods. There aren't many of these, of course. But familiar hunting grounds or good fishing spots on the river are what most focus on rather than "adventuring sites." Villagers almost always keep to the known paths and trails, and know various landmarks that others might not take note of, like a particularly twisted tree, an odd shaped boulder, and so on. And of course, everyone knows that when in doubt, if you're lost in the woods, you can get to the river and follow it (usually upstream, unless you're at Lake Memory) to get back home, or navigate by looking to the steep valley walls, which are practically always in sight.

WRAPPING UP

As previously mentioned, the campaign will likely take the characters to tier 3. At that point, either the Uldada has been stopped or it is complete, and thus Neandran is either saved or destroyed. Essatha is either defeated (which probably means dead) or she's escaped through the completed Uldada into . . . who knows where.

Obviously, the PCs are free to remain in the valley as long as they wish. Cleaning up the damage done to Neandran is a big task, not to mention Ketterach, a place that either just barely fended off invasion or fell to the siege. Ketterach in particular certainly has more opportunities for adventure (criminals, politics, and the underwater caves, just for starters).

Or, like birds leaving the nest, the characters might leave the Glimmering Valley and explore the world beyond. The opportunities are limitless out there.

CREATING CHARACTERS FOR THE GLIMMERING VALLEY

Character Types,
page 28

Cyphers, page 272

Oddities, page 304

*Folks don't know that
the dream is based on
prior-world civilizations
and technology, so
they don't think of
it as magical.*

Character Creation in
Ketterach, page 90

Descriptors, page 53

Cultured, page 43

Village Connections,
page 20

Starting PCs are from Neandran. Since Numenera is a broad game offering options for a wide variety of backgrounds, that means some special considerations are in play.

Character creation is limited to *Discovery* types at first: Glaive, Nano, and Jack. The people of the little isolated village have no experience with the abilities of other types, such as those found in *Destiny*. The Wright and the Delve require a strong connection to making numenera devices and going into dangerous places, which are essentially unknown in Neandran. Arkai are expected to be community leaders from the start, and in the Glimmering Valley campaign, that's a role we want characters to work for rather than begin with.

However, players that want to play a Wright, an Arkus, or a Delve can do so with a new character once the flow of the campaign reaches the small city Ketterach at the other end of the valley, where they are introduced to the concepts. Alternatively, an existing character can transition to a new type once they get there. Either way, should they bring these new concepts and abilities back to Neandran, they can eventually be hailed as the village's first Wright, Arkus, or Delve.

Any descriptor is available for characters except for Cultured. Rather than a connection to the starting adventure that every descriptor normally provides, however, each character has one or more village connections.

SPECIAL ABILITIES AND THE NUMENERA

The people of Neandran consider leftovers from the prior worlds to be, unquestionably, magic. And most magic is thought to be dangerous at best, and outright evil at worst. Thus, devices like cyphers and even oddities are relatively rare in the village. Leaving Neandran to seek more isn't directly discouraged, but neither is it encouraged. The village has a complicated relationship with "magic."

Very rarely, some of the children of Neandran are born with strange mutations thanks to a low level of unknown energy from the crystal monoliths flanking the village. People like Easchel, an outspoken opponent of anything "magical," refer to these mutations as sorcery and consider their existence as dangerous at best. In the past, accidents and misuse of "sorcery" have resulted in damage to the village and loss of life. Some with sorcerous powers have been exiled from Neandran for the good of the village.

While wise folk know that the crystals give off these transmutative energies, they also know that the same emanations enhance the crops and livestock in the village, and even help keep the water supply pure. They quietly advised the people of Neandran to stay despite the occasional experiences with dangerous sorcery.

In other words, those in the know realize that the numenera is a mixed bag for the village. And a few people—some of them influential and vocal—believe it to be much too dangerous to tolerate. So, both devices and abilities arising from the numenera remain rare.

It's thematically appropriate to have a group of PCs in which no more than half wield dramatic, "magic" powers. Neandran is a quiet, unassuming little village and such things are not common there.

DISCOVERY FOCI IN NEANDRAN

Bears a Halo of Fire: A rare mutation is likely the source for these fire-related powers. Such dramatic displays of "sorcery" will certainly get the attention of Easchel.

Commands Mental Powers: Another result of a rare birth mutation, the abilities granted by this focus are perhaps subtle enough that Easchel will not have noticed.

Controls Beasts: This focus doesn't have to represent anything more than a strong affinity for animals—although its benefits are nigh uncanny, they don't need to be "supernatural." Until tier 4, that is. At that point, even a "mundane" beast master has gained the power of Beast Eyes. Of course, if the player wishes, the abilities can also be the result of mutation from the get-go.

Controls Gravity: Like Bears a Halo of Fire, this is a mutation with overt effects. Easchel will eye such a character suspiciously.

Crafts Illusions: This kind of overt "sorcery" would panic most people in Neandran.

Employs Magnetism: Like Bears a Halo of Fire, this is a mutation with overt effects. Easchel will eye such a character suspiciously.

Entertains: Although someone who is entertaining can come from a variety of backgrounds, it's quite possible that a character with this focus is a protege of Aryle. Perhaps they are still friends, or perhaps they had a falling-out and are more like rivals.

Exists Partially Out of Phase: Someone exercising such powers would likely be seen as trafficking with ghosts and spirits, and feared.

Explores Dark Places: At worst, this character might be seen as a bit quirky. They probably know the Empty Caves quite well.

Fights With Panache: People might find this character ostentatious, but they would be easily accepted in the village. They'd probably be familiar with Kyath, perhaps even having learned from him.

Focuses Mind Over Matter: Like Bears a Halo of Fire, this is a mutation with overt effects. Easchel will eye such a character suspiciously.

Fuses Flesh and Steel: This is a popular choice among foci (who doesn't want to be a cyborg at least once?) but sadly it would be very difficult to fit such a character into Neandran. No one in the village has the know-how to create and maintain such systems, and nothing nearby would explain it either. However, there is an encounter in the Ancient Crèche that could give someone this focus, and if the PCs travel to Ketterach, a player can then start a new character with this focus as well.

Howls at the Moon: A character with this focus is asking for some headaches, because the beast they turn into would be hunted and (if found) destroyed.

Hunts: This well-accepted character likely knows and has some kind of relationship to Mert.

Lives in the Wilderness: This well-accepted character likely knows and has some kind of relationship to Mert.

Masters Defense: This character probably trained with Kyath.

Masters Weaponry: This character probably trained with Kyath.

Murders: Neandran is far too small and remote to have any truck with a professional killer. This is not an appropriate starting focus.

Rages: Although people in Neandran might be a little wary of a character that loses control, there's no reason they wouldn't be accepted.

Rides the Lightning: A rare mutation is likely the source for these electrical powers. Such dramatic displays of "sorcery" will certainly get the attention of Easchel.

Speaks With a Silver Tongue: This well-accepted character might be a protege or friend of Aryle.

Talks to Machines: There aren't a lot of machines to practice on, but a character with this focus would certainly have incentive to explore!

Wears a Sheen of Ice: Like Bears a Halo of Fire, this is a mutation with overt effects. Easchel will eye such a character suspiciously.

Foci, page 58

Easchel, page 24

Ancient Crèche, page 61

Mert, page 27

Kyath, page 26

Aryle, page 24

Empty Caves, page 43

Wields Power With Precision: There's no one to teach a character these abilities in Neandran.

Wields Two Weapons at Once: This character may have trained with Kyath.

Works the Back Alleys: While thievery is not unknown in Neandran, there are no full-time, professional criminals there. The bandits near the town, such as Belof and Echealli, could be considered such folk, but as is obvious, they were thrown out of the village (or left on their own). This is probably not an appropriate focus for a starting PC.

Belof and Echealli, page 37

Works Miracles: While probably another mutation that appears like sorcery, the beneficial effects of this focus make this character a beloved member of society in the village. Even Easchel's suspicions won't sway public opinion on this matter. Instead, Verge might be convinced to reluctantly train a young person with such talents to help with his work.

Verge, page 28

Foci, page 55

DESTINY FOCI IN NEANDRAN

Absorbs Energy: Clearly supernatural powers, the abilities granted by this focus will draw the attention of Easchel.

Acts Without Consequence: Troublemakers have a tough go in the village, but this focus is probably a better fit than Works the Back Alleys.

Adjures the Leviathan: "Leviathan" isn't much of a Neandran-style term, but "Calms the Beast" might fit better. This could easily be used on a variety of beasts in the woods.

Augments Flesh With Grafts: It would be extremely difficult for such a character to begin in Neandran, in terms of materials and tools, not to mention in terms of community acceptance.

Amrose, page 23

Battles Automatons: Automatons are rare in and around the village, to say the least. Not appropriate for a starting PC.

Brandishes an Exotic Shield: This likely exists due to a mutation one might be born with. Such dramatic displays of "sorcery" will certainly get the attention of Easchel.

Sesson, page 28

Breaks Down Walls: Given the supernatural nature of the strength this focus imparts, it would need to be hidden from Easchel.

Luttan, page 26
Jofan, page 26
Ulam, page 27

Builds Tomorrow: No one in the village has the knowledge about building devices to provide the understanding and context needed. Not for starting characters.

Dances With Dark Matter: The sinister undercurrents of this focus make it a poor fit for characters starting in Neandran.

Defends the Gate: Probably a student of Kyath, this is a perfect fit for any warrior who wants to defend the village.

Defends the Weak: As with Defends the Gate, it is a perfect fit for any warrior who wants to defend the village who and is a student of Kyath.

Descends From Nobility: No one in Neandran traces their lineage or considers their family nobility, so this is not appropriate for a starting character.

Emerged From the Obelisk: A character with this focus has their origin tied directly to the crystal monoliths in the village. Obviously, their crystalline body is going to cause a stir in the village, and they'll be branded a demon by Easchel.

Explores Yesterday: At worst, this character might be seen as a bit quirky. They probably know the Empty Caves quite well.

Fights With a Horde: There are no fighting societies in Neandran with which a starting character could have trained.

Fuses Mind and Machine: Like Fuses Flesh and Steel, this probably isn't appropriate for a starting character in Neandran.

Hunts Abhumans: There are no abhumans in the valley. Yet. (See Chapter 11: The Ourach Invasion.)

Imparts Wisdom: Arguably, Amrose could have taken this character under her wing and imparted some of her thoughts. It's likely that a knowledge-seeking character such as this would be eager to leave the village.

Leads: Some folks are just born leaders. Such a person may have been groomed by Amrose or Sesson in Neandran.

Learns From Adversity: This focus is well-suited to village life, and the character would likely have some kind of kinship with a person or persons there who likewise have learned from experience, such as Mert, Kyath, Luttan, or even Jofan or Ulam.

Metes Out Justice: With few codified laws and no lawkeepers in Neandran, this is probably not an appropriate starting focus.

Moves Like a Cat: Odet, despite her age, could instruct a younger person in the ways of this focus, as could Aryle. It could also just be something that comes naturally to a PC.

Needs No Weapons: Odet, despite her age, is enough of a skilled brawler that she could train someone how to handle themselves in a fight without weapons.

Never Says Die: This could just be something that comes naturally to the PC, although someone like Mert, Odet, Kyath, or perhaps even Verge could provide help or insight.

Possesses a Shard of the Sun: As this involves a prior world leftover, it's probably not appropriate for people born in Neandran.

Radiates Vitality: This is a mutation with overt effects. Easchel will eye such a character suspiciously.

Sees Beyond: Although they're concealed easily enough, the abilities granted by this focus came as a mutation from the crystal monoliths. Easchel will call this character a sorcerer if he finds out about the ability.

Shepherds the Community: This person would likely be well-liked throughout the village, and Amrose and Aryle might have taken them under their collective wings.

Shreds the Walls of the World: Like Exists Partially Out of Phase, someone exercising such powers would likely be seen as trafficking with ghosts and spirits, and feared.

Thunders: A mutation from the crystal monoliths is likely the source for these powers. Such dramatic displays of "sorcery" will certainly get the attention of Easchel.

Touches the Sky: A mutation from crystal monoliths is likely the source for these powers. Such dramatic displays of "sorcery" will certainly get the attention of Easchel.

Wields Words Like Weapons: This well-accepted character might be a protégé or friend of Aryle.

Odet, page 27

Aryle, page 24

17

EQUIPMENT AVAILABLE IN NEANDRAN

Equipment, page 93

Most of the common armors, weapons, and equipment are available to starting characters, although it's worth noting that heavy weapons and armor are extremely uncommon and probably have a story behind them, like they were originally bought from a traveling merchant or inherited from a relative.

Even chainmail is fairly uncommon, with medium armor made from beastskin being much more prevalent.

Special armors are not available.

Folks in the village can craft most basic objects, and in particular Neandran boasts some excellent woodcrafters. Thus, metal tools and weapons are certainly not unknown, but are more treasured objects there (metal comes from outside the village exclusively).

Common special equipment is available, but all are as precious and rare, or rarer, than metal regardless of their composition. No one in Neandran is crafting synth bags, compasses, or ink pens. These would all have come through trade with traveling merchants or perhaps someone in the past doing some exploring.

Rare and very rare special equipment is not available at the start of the campaign, but can be purchased in Ketterach.

MONEY AND WEALTH

The folk of Neandran keep shins for use with traders from outside the village, and such folk only make occasional appearances—usually no more than once each month, and sometimes less. Within the village, goods are not bought or sold, but distributed as needed. A woman named

Luttan, however, is no fool. If adventurous characters are off to Ketterach and suddenly "need" goods valuable in the city, she knows they're taking them to sell. Rather than refusing, however, she'll tally up what the characters should get by trading the goods, and tell them she expects them to return with an equal amount of goods the village needs. In fact, she'll give them a shopping list.

Ketterach, page 84

CYPHERS

As previously stated, cyphers are rare in Neandran. Beginning characters start with one fewer than their cypher limit. These starting cyphers likely represent something they or their family have hoarded for some time, for when it's most needed. Of course, PCs that head off in search of adventure are sure to quickly discover that devices like cyphers are much more plentiful than they've been led to believe.

Alternatively, a GM could start each PC with their full allotment of cyphers, assuming at least half of those cyphers are "natural." That is to say, concoctions brewed by Atta, the so-called Old Witch outside of town, or simply potent herbs, roots, and so on gathered by the PCs (or others).

*Cypher Dangers,
page 272*

Atta, page 39

Luttan keeps careful track of what everyone produces and keeps in the storehouses. She likewise knows what people need and does whatever she can to see that they get it. As a community without a formal leader, Neandran is also a community without any concept of social class or individualized wealth. When times are good, everyone prospers equally, and when things go poorly, all the residents suffer together.

This means that if a PC needs something, they can more than likely just get it. The problem isn't cost, but availability.

Luttan keeps things fair and evenly distributed. No one should ask for more than they can legitimately use—and truthfully, what would be the point of doing so anyway? The villagers all know that they can get what they need (if it's available) so there's no need to hoard.

NAMES

People of Neandran don't use surnames. A single, usually one- or two-syllable name is most common, often with moderately soft sounds like Amrose or Luttan. The only person with a hard K in their name is Kyath, and he's not originally from the village. Names are not tied to a gender or status.

Names usually cycle through the generations in a family, but never while the original name holder is alive. So Thear had a grandfather named Thear, and her parents named her because he had already passed by the time she was born. Her family won't name a child Thear again until she has, in turn, passed. Reusing the name of an ancestor is always meant to be a way of honoring the past.

Allow players to give their characters any single name they wish.

Luttan, page 26

FAMILIES AND FRIENDS

All but the most misanthropic PCs are going to have family and friends in Neandran. Working with the GM, each player should choose at least one and perhaps as many as five or six of the NPCs from the village, found in Chapter 3: Neandran. The PC is either related to or particularly friendly with these characters, perhaps even living in the same house as they do.

The village's population far exceeds those named NPCs, however, so there is ample room for new characters to be added as needed. For example, a character might know Veri and Yurran as they grew up right next door, and thus by extension they might know Amrose and Aryle (Veri's parents) fairly well, but the PC's actual parents are NPCs of the player's creation. This mixture of existing NPCs and those inserted as needed provides a nice feeling of connection to the community for each player, so GMs should absolutely not miss this opportunity.

Family and friends offer a way to explain the equipment and cyphers a PC starts with, and perhaps the training they have in their skills and abilities. Encourage both comparing and contrasting NPCs with the PCs. That is to say, a PC who is friends with Luttan might be very well organized, smart, and devoted to the village, but they might also be friends with (the disorderly) Mert. Our friends sometimes complement our outlook, but they sometimes also provide interesting foils. Imagine the awkward situation where a PC who Bears a Halo of Fire lives next door to Easchel. Or perhaps Easchel is their father!

People of Importance, page 23

NPCs in the village can offer advice and maybe a story or two about the world, but they aren't there to send the PCs off on quests.

Veri and Yurran, page 23

Amrose, page 23

Aryle, page 24

Luttan, page 26

Mert, page 27

Easchel, page 24

Ien, page 31

Alloise, page 25

Ketterach, page 84

The idea here isn't to encourage the PCs to never leave. Rather, it's to show how important the village is to the characters.

Easchel

Mert

VILLAGE CONNECTIONS

Above and beyond knowing who their friends and family in Neandran are, each PC should have a special link to one of the named NPCs. Each player should pick a person in the village to have this strong connection to their PC. And there should be a narrative reason for the connection that ties in with the PC's background.

Once per day (once between ten-hour rests), the player can make the equivalent of a player intrusion but with no XP cost. However, the intrusion must relate to the connected NPC from the village.

For example:

- [Connected NPC] has the tool I need and happens to walk by so I can ask them for it.
- [Connected NPC] knows the cure for this malady and will share it with me.
- [Connected NPC] will hide us for the evening in their house.

The connection, of course, has the most value when the players are in the village. In the valley outside the village, the connection can be called upon in less direct ways. Such intrusions might be linked to advice, gifts, or tiny bits of knowledge that happen to be useful in a given situation. Examples:

- [Connected NPC] told me about a plant that grows in deep gullies that might treat this poison.
- [Connected NPC] once mentioned these beasts and that they have an aversion to water.
- [Connected NPC] gave me this tool we need before we left the village.
- [Connected NPC] once showed me a trick to fix a broken bow like this.

Obviously, the intrusion has to fit the NPC as well as the situation. Ien could have shared insight about the best place to ford the river, but Easchel, who has never left Neandran, couldn't. Likewise, Alloise is unlikely to have had a rock-crafting tool to give the PC, but they might have given them something more suited to leatherworking.

However, by the time the PCs reach Ketterach, the special connection ability can be drawn upon every other day. And if the PCs leave the valley entirely, the connection cannot be called upon. Returning to the village restores the ability.

INDIVIDUAL INFORMATION

Once connections have been determined, the GM should give one of the following pieces of information to each character. The information probably comes from their connected NPC, but in some cases, a different source might be appropriate. All of these bits of lore and rumors are true.

- There are places along the valley walls where you can find caves that grant access to the ancient structures that compose the walls.
- Somewhere out in the woods there is a metal staircase that goes up to nowhere.
- The Old Witch has many secrets, and knows many things about the valley that others do not.
- Some criminals and ruffians living in a camp out in the woods have been known to cause trouble. There've been some sightings of them in and around Neandran in the last week.
- Some folks in the village think that the new dream is a portent of something terrible, and has to do with something that started ages ago in the distant past.
- There are people in the village who are hiding something. It could be some strange sorcery, or it could be something else.
- Because there haven't really been many explorers in a generation, the valley holds many places still unexplored.

Luttan

Verge

GETTING STARTED

Once characters are created, players are granted full agency to decide what to do. The Uldada has not appeared yet, so they can explore the lake, deal with the "bandits," visit the Old Witch, or do whatever else they like.

No one tells them what to do or where to go. In fact, most people would likely discourage brazenly heading into the wilderness. The PCs are likely among the best and the brightest of their generation in the village where gifted youngsters are a precious resource.

If the players are utterly stumped for anything to do, the following small tasks could use their help.

- A young herder (a typical villager by the name of Soort) says that a gobrin has wandered off and got lost and they need help finding it. This could lead to a valley encounter for the PCs.
- Verge needs an elixir from the Old Witch and sends the PCs to procure it.
- Luttan asks the PCs to gather some ustis seeds in the woods, as the supply is getting low and they should just be coming into season. Ustis seeds are simply a spice, but one that everyone enjoys, and finding them could lead to a valley encounter.
- Rystan asks the PCs for help. Her neighbor has become sick. He's a man named Lege and he is going through withdrawal from Belof's drug, having used an herbal hair-growth serum from Bedor laced with the stuff. No one knows these are withdrawal symptoms, but it's not hard to find Bedor, and it's not hard to convince him to reveal the scheme put forth by Belof and Echealli.

Once the Uldada appears, however, the need for the PCs to act becomes more urgent.

Rystan

Gobrin, page 23

Valley Encounters, page 44

Verge, page 28

Rystan, page 27

Bedor, page 24

Belof and Echealli, page 37

Uldada, page 93

NEANDRAN

Four hundred and thirty-two people live in and around Neandran. A few dozen buildings of clay and wood surround a single, ancient structure and a pair of crystal monoliths nestled amid the thick growth of the forest. Nearby, some land has been cleared for crops and grazing animals, but in general the village feels quite hidden and protected.

CULTURE

Neandran has fifty-one extended families. About a quarter of the population is under the age of 16, at which age people are considered adults.

Most families in the village live together or in very close proximity. Children grow up as close to their uncles, aunts, and grandparents as to their parents. They eke out a living raising small crops, tending to a small stock of animals, and hunting and gathering in the woods. A few skilled craftspeople work with stone, clay, and wood. It's a communal society, and as long as someone pulls their own weight, the community ensures that they are fed, sheltered, and have what they need. Technically people barter for goods and services, but most don't even pay attention to such things unless someone tries to take advantage.

The folk here have, without exception, never left the Glimmering Valley. However, while the topography does make it hard to leave, the people of Neandran stay where they are by choice. Most enjoy their quiet life in the woods, content to live out their days in the village and the surrounding area without ever traveling more than a few miles from the spot where they were

Thates, page 23

Sarrata, page 116
Veeshin, page 119

born. The bravest and most adventurous (probably propelled by their youth) might head into the woods to find the Dreaming Cubes, see the River Ring, or maybe visit the Old Witch in the Infinite Abode. The true explorers, filled with wanderlust, must travel the length of the valley to Ketterach. While some stay in the "big city," most return to the peace and simplicity of the village. The very select few head out into the greater world beyond, never to come back to Neandran again.

The village does get the occasional visitor. Three or four times each year, during the summer or autumn when the weather's good, a trader will bring a cart down the paths filled with goods unavailable in Neandran: sugar, spices, metal, and perhaps a little synth. The trader likely leaves with thates, wool, and wood, happy to have made the trades. The woods are dangerous, though, and a wise trader probably brings a guard or two with them to fend off sarrata, veeshin, or robbers.

THE SUPERNATURAL

To the people of Neandran, the numenera is magic. Gods and demons are the source of the various strange things encountered in the valley, and superstitions are considered fact. The dream that everyone shares is a remnant of a great war fought by ancient gods—and they assume it affects the entire world.

While not everyone in Neandran is religious, all of those who are—at least openly—revere Loe as their patron and protector. The ancient structure at the village center serves as a temple to this god, believed to be a protective and nurturing spirit. There is, however, a much more

secretive and sinister supernatural belief system lurking in the shadows. A small group of individuals has fallen under the sway of Illace, who secretly worships the Uttarek—her name for the "demons" within the Dreaming Cubes. She and her followers slip out on particular nights to perform rather ghastly rites at that ancient site.

DOMESTICATED ANIMALS

The folk of the village keep seskii as pets and companions, particularly the herders and woodcutters, who use them for protection, fitted with collars spiked with bone.

Gobrin are shaggy grey goats. Fully half of gobrin born in the village are born in conjoined pairs, meaning that they have two heads, and sometimes six legs. Herders and everyone else know that this is quite common, and do not see these specimens as unviable or aberrations. In fact, most live the same healthy lives as their single-headed brethren.

FOOD

Thates—hardy, starchy tubers—serve as the foundation of the Neandran diet. Bread made of flour from ground thates and stuffed with cooked thates, spices, and meat is a staple.

The forest offers a variety of berries, wild fruit, leaves, wild tubers, mushrooms, and other edible flora at different times of year, and the folks in Neandran know how, where, and when to gather them all.

While herders keep flocks of gobrin, this is mainly for the milk and the wool. Most meat comes from small game trapped or hunted. The forest teems with a wide variety of life.

PEOPLE OF IMPORTANCE

Neandran has no official leader—no mayor or reeve—and nothing akin to an aristocracy. Everyone in the village is treated as an equal, and everyone has a voice. That doesn't mean that everyone agrees or gets along, however.

AMROSE

Some people are just natural leaders. Despite having no real authority, when a decision needs to be made, people turn to Amrose. Some even refer to her as Amrose the Wise, although she doesn't care for it.

Amrose is neither physically impressive nor imposing. She uses simple, straightforward language, and while she might seem a little stern and she never makes a joke, she appreciates humor and good spirits. This is likely what has fostered the relationship she has with her partner, Aryle.

She and Aryle have a grown daughter, Veri, who is married to Yurran. They both work as bakers in the village.

Amrose

Dreaming Cubes, page 42

Seskii, page 252

Gobrin: level 2; Armor 1

Amrose: level 5, level 7 for all matters concerning wise decisions, level 6 for social skills (including seeing through deception)

USING THE COMMUNITY RULES FROM DESTINY

Neandran is a rank 1 community, with 3 health but an infrastructure rating of 5 thanks to the temple and the crystal monoliths. It has no other special modifications.

The Uldada is a rank 5 disaster and it doubles the damage against infrastructure. It can only be dealt with by the PCs as described in Chapter 10: The Uldada.

There really are no creatures in the valley that could be considered a rampaging beast. Should the ourachs reach Neandran, however, they would form a marauding horde of rank 4 (and thus would wipe the village out fairly quickly).

While general long-term tasks could be accomplished in the village, most of the long-term task examples based on type might not be appropriate for Neandran, although glaives could train defenders and teach martial skills there. Most long-term tasks would be better accomplished in Ketterach.

The Uldada, page 93
Ourach, page 100

Disasters, page 308
Hordes, page 312
Long-Term Tasks, page 324

ARYLE

Loquacious and energetic, Aryle is a born entertainer. He's more likely to sing the answer to a question than say it, more likely to dance his way down a stretch of road than just walk. He's a bright spirit in the village and affable with almost all. Although he happily helps out wherever he's needed, Aryle's role in Neandran is that of storyteller and entertainer. He organizes any parties or celebrations in the village, teaches young folk the art of dance and song, and conducts similar duties. He is loved by all. Aryle is lanky and bald, almost always smiling or whistling. He dresses in bright, surprising colors, but you wouldn't call him flamboyant.

Aryle

Aryle: *level 5, level 7 for entertaining, level 6 for all other social skills*

Bedor: *level 2, level 3 for stealth, level 1 for resisting intimidation or trickery*

Bedor is not listed in the Player's Guide.

Easchel: *level 4, level 5 for perception*

Bik: *level 3, level 4 for pleasant social interaction, cooking, and brewing; level 2 for anything physical*

Belof and Echealli, page 37

BEDOR

A younger cousin of Belof and Echealli, Bedor is a weasel of a young man, always shirking work and responsibility. However, his criminal cousins have roped him into their scheme to try to get some of the villagers addicted to a narcotic that they make, so those villagers are then beholden to them. It's a terrible scheme and will likely fall apart quickly, but Bedor's role is to offer people some herbal concoctions from the Old Witch laced with the drug.

Bedor is skinny and dresses slovenly. He is weak in both will and wit. Everyone knows that Bedor is cousins with Belof and Echealli, and they know he interacts with them on the sly. Although his mother, a herder named Koral, tries her best with him, everyone quietly expects that Bedor will end up a full-time member of their pathetic little band. He knows the way to their camp down by the river.

Easchel

BICHEL (BIK)

Bik runs the Post, the village's gathering spot. He serves drinks and food (that he prepares) and makes everyone feel welcome and comfortable. He sees that as his contribution to the village, and folks universally agree that he and the Post make the village a better place. No one dislikes Bik.

He brews thates alcohol in a contraption behind the Post.

Broad in face and chest, Bik stands just below average height. His clothes are usually stained with whatever food he's been preparing, or even what he was preparing over the last few days. He's always got a smile for everyone and he's often singing a delightful song that he's just made up on the spot. He's no good in a fight, or really any sort of crisis, but that's not what people expect from him.

EASCHEL

Tall and gaunt, Easchel proudly states that he's never taken a step outside of Neandran. He advocates for the "old ways" in all things, insisting that a "tried and true" method or explanation exists for everything. To Easchel, the old ways are key to a simple village life. But the old ways remain under constant threat of diabolic sorcery. And to be certain, anything he thinks is surprising, odd, or suspicious is sorcery.

Easchel's outlook may seem confusing to the players, who know that the prior worlds are the source of the numenera. The prior worlds are not the old ways that he refers to. Easchel rejects terms like the "prior worlds" and "numenera." To him, the ages before humanity were simply an era of darkness and evil—the things left behind are the wreckage of the demons' own bitter end they brought upon themselves. If people wouldn't go digging them up, they would stay buried, and the world would be safe. The old ways, then, are not ancient; they are from the time of his grandparents, or perhaps their parents. He refuses to think about an era before that.

His predecessors taught him that sorcery was not just to be avoided, but to be stamped out should it ever make its way into the lives of good, upstanding folk. This is why he remains vigilant in looking for those who would wield supernatural powers or utilize ancient devices in any way. For the PCs, this means type or focus abilities that are overtly "sorcerous," or the use of the numenera.

The source of most of the sorcery, according to Easchel, is the city of Ketterach at the other end of the valley. Or, as he calls it, "the city of devils" or, when he's feeling charitable, "the city of the bird-men." (Easchel heard tell of the Parahawks there and became convinced that at least some of the inhabitants are inhuman bird-people.)

GONNOR

Gonnor works with stone and occasionally metal. Just outside his house stands his impressive workshop filled with the village's largest number of tools. His work is known more for its quality than its beauty, a fact that he's constantly apologizing for, although no one ever seems to feel it necessary. Because metal only comes from outside the village, Gonnor doesn't forge many items, and instead repairs those iron and steel items that folks have when they're needed.

Gonnor is unfortunately given to long bouts of depression. His family does their best to help, but what happens is that Gonnor disappears for days at a time. His partner Alloise has learned to deal with it and has grown accustomed to taking care of their three children by herself. Her real fear is that one day he won't return.

Gonnor

ILLACE

Most know Illace as a tailor and a cook. She's friendly and liked, although for the most part she draws little attention to herself. At least to the eyes of most. The truth is, Illace leads a secret cult in the village that worships the creatures trapped in the Dreaming Cubes. She has named these entities the Uttarek, and believes that if she can free them, they will grant her eternal life and other blessings.

Illace can create blinding light or make the area around her extremely dim. She believes that the strange control over light she's had from birth is a blessing from the Uttarek, and that it is a sign from them that she is chosen to work on their behalf. This is, of course, nonsense—she gained her abilities via mutation from the crystal monoliths and the beings in the Dreaming Cubes have no way of communicating with her, or even knowing she exists.

Over the years, Illace has managed to find a handful of others in Neandran that hold similar desires, and converted them to the worship of the Uttarek. She is extremely careful when doing so, for she knows that if her secret devotion got out, she would be exiled from the village. Her cult now involves five locals other than herself. They gather at least once a month at night and venture out to the Dreaming Cubes to pray to their adopted masters.

They have little fear of detection thanks to a concoction brewed for them by Atta, the Old Witch. This herbal mixture allows them to move in the shadows with ease and make almost no noise (easing stealth by 2 steps for 10 minutes).

The cult does not possess any knowledge of how the Uttarek might be released, but Illace prays every night for some kind of vision or key. (The key exists in the form of the Lost Cube, but she is unaware of it.)

Illace is small and stout, with curly grey hair. In the secret pockets she's sewn into her clothes, she hides a knife, three doses of level 5 poison (inflicts 5 points of Speed damage), and a level 4 cypher that appears

Illace

For abilities Easchel would find objectionable, see the section on special abilities starting on page 14.

Gonnor: *level 4, level 5 for stonecrafting and metalworking*

Atta, page 39

The Lost Cube, page 47

Illace: *level 5, level 7 for stealth and deception including sudden unexpected attacks, level 4 for physical actions including combat (excluding surprise attacks); can create blinding light or very dim light in an immediate area; has a poisoned knife and a level 4 amnesia gas bomb cypher*

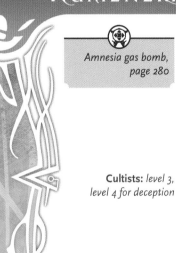

Amnesia gas bomb, page 280

Cultists: level 3, level 4 for deception

Belof and Echealli, page 37

Sarrat, page 116

Kyath: level 5, level 7 for attacks and damage with weapons; health 20; Armor 2

Luttan: level 3; level 5 for management; level 4 for all social skills, including seeing through deception

Jofan: level 3

to be a short synth rod with a cube at one end that produces amnesia gas within an immediate area. She can also use her blinding light power to blind anyone in an immediate area that is not prepared (Illace, obviously, knows to be prepared if she uses this, and even has a warning phrase, "bright blessings," that she has shared with her fellow cultists so that they won't be affected either).

If anyone were to search Illace's house, they would find a journal she keeps with sketches of the creatures that can be seen in the Dreaming Cubes, although one would have to have visited the cubes to make the connection. Some of the pages are labeled "Uttarek." One page says, "We must free them. We must find a key." She also writes a little about her powers and her status as being the sacred chosen one. On the cover of the journal, she has written "Bright Blessings."

JOFAN

Born with a mutation as a result of the crystal monoliths, Jofan's face is misshapen— the left side of his face moreso than the right. His arm is scarred and he walks with a slight limp. Unlike some of the others affected by the monoliths' energies, he has no special abilities or adaptations.

Jofan is amiable and well-liked around Neandran. He helps around the village doing odd jobs.

KYATH

Kyath was born in Ketterach. As a young man, he served as a guard for a merchant and eventually accompanied a trader that went to and from Neandran. A few years ago, he decided to stay in the village to settle down. Meeting the love of his life there, a woman named Udya, probably played a part in that decision.

Kyath owns his own chainmail hauberk and his own steel blade. Neither has much use in his current life as a farmer, but occasionally he has to pick both up again if some threat to Neandran rears its head. He'll teach an apt pupil the art of defense, or the use of a sword or other weapon, but he's quite modest about his own skills— which are formidable. If Belof and Echealli started causing serious trouble for the villagers, or a sarrat attacked, most people would look to Kyath to lead any efforts to protect them.

Getting on toward middle age, Kyath's belly is a little rounder and his hair is a little thinner, but he's as quick and strong as he ever was. Kyath and Udya have three children, all quite young.

LUTTAN

If a villager in Neandran needs something, they go to Luttan. She manages essentially all of Neandran's resources. She works out barter deals on people's behalf when possible, but also just ensures that no one goes without. For example, when the aging

Kyath

Jofan

Luttan

widow Ulam has run out of firewood, she'll talk to woodcutter Narth about getting some to her, perhaps in exchange for some nicely baked bread. And if Ulam isn't up to baking, Luttan will procure three new blankets from Deke the weaver to give Narth on Ulam's behalf.

Luttan has access to the village's storehouses and apportions out goods as she sees fit. She also uses these communal goods to conduct trade with those bringing in goods from outside the village.

Luttan is surprisingly young for the level of trust and confidence essentially everyone has in her. She doesn't allow the malformed leg she was born with to slow down her tireless efforts, but her limp definitely becomes more obvious as the day wears on.

She is in love with Navrati, the firstborn of Thear and Messos. They plan to marry soon, as soon as Thear and Messos grant their blessing.

MERT

No one knows the woods around Neandran like Mert. She's tracked rean, snared nobba, and chased baroon through every thicket, grove, gully, and glade for miles. Mert is stocky and solid, pushing middle age, and her face and clothes are always stained with something—dirt, mud, sap, or worse. She hardly notices.

Skilled with a bow and a knife, Mert has hunted or trapped almost anything worth hunting or trapping in the valley. But she's neither sadistic nor cruel. She brings meat and skins from her kills to the village to be used by all, and she often makes tools or art with the bones.

Mert is in Neandran occasionally. Usually, she's out in the woods. When she does come to town, she's known as a heavy drinker and a mean drunk, but boastful and loud even when sober. Still, people respect her and appreciate her talents. It's likely that she will need to one day contend with her alcoholism.

ODET

Odet oversees the mill. The mill is a bit of a walk from the village, but Odet says the daily walk keeps her young. She's unimposing, but her build and her age shouldn't be mistaken for signs of weakness or frailty.

Odet has a reputation around Neandran as a brawler. She claims that those days are behind her, but if Mert is in town it's not uncommon for she and Odet to get into a shouting match if Mert gets drunk, and shouts turn into punches and kicks.

Odet's vitality and strength come in part from the energies of the crystal monoliths, but she doesn't know that, and wouldn't believe you if you told her.

RYSTAN

Rystan works as a glassblower, as her older brother did before he died in an accident. Attractive and slim, Rystan would rather be socializing (and gossiping) than working. Her work is adequate, but it's clearly not of great importance to her. She does, by many accounts, "snoop" about the town, and delights in knowing people's private matters.

Rystan and Thear's husband Messos had a brief tryst a few years ago, and while Thear has forgiven her husband she neither trusts nor likes Rystan. The two do not conceal their contempt for each other.

Odet

Odet: *level 4; level 5 for unarmed combat, including damage*

Rystan: *level 3, level 4 for perception*

Rean, page 115
Nobba, page 35
Baroon, page 109

Mert: *level 6; level 7 for hunting, trapping, and tracking; health 25; Armor 2*

Mert

Rystan

Sesson: *level 4, level 5 for pleasant social skills and religious knowledge*

Thear: *level 3, level 5 for woodworking*

Messos: *level 3*
Navrati: *level 2, level 3 for woodworking*
Lym: *level 2*

Other Neandran villagers: *level 2*

Ien: *level 3, level 4 for fishing*

Verge: *level 3, level 5 for healing, level 4 for herbology and biology, level 2 for pleasant social interaction; healing in his care occurs at 3 times the normal rate*

SESSON

Sesson serves as the priest of Loe in the temple. Of average height and build, his eyes sparkle with life and good humor. Gregarious and outgoing, Sesson is quick to help those around him with a hand, a kind word, or a bit of advice. He sees himself as a representative of Loe—a caring and kind deity, according to the doctrines—and thus a figure of responsibility rather than authority over the other villagers. There's no proselytizing in his religion, no guilt or shame, and no long list of sins. Instead, it's focused mainly in seeing the blessings of Loe, focusing on their nurturing and caring nature, and acting in kind as a mortal follower. In addition to helping those in need, Sesson's role includes observing holy days (which are frequent) and leading religious rituals in the temple.

Sesson's husband is named Ien and he is a river fisherman, spending most of his days tending nets.

THEAR

If you live in Neandran and have furniture in your house with even the slightest bit of style, it was probably made by Thear (or her father). Thear is a woodworker with an artistic flair whose family has been focused on woodcraft for generations. She is rather nondescript in appearance, usually wearing a thick apron with a variety of loops and pockets for tools. She smells of sawdust and lacquer.

Thear is married to Messos, and they have two children, Navrati and Lym. Navrati works as his mother's assistant, and Lym might as well, when he is older. Messos is a broad-shouldered man a few years younger than Thear, kept busy providing wood for his wife's work.

VERGE

Verge likes no one, but takes care of everyone. Gruff and surly, everything is always an effort, it would seem, and yet he never says no. It's an open secret that Verge has a sort of "magic touch" when it comes to healing wounds. In his care, serious wounds quickly become minor wounds and recovery from illnesses often happens faster than expected. No one, however, talks about Verge that way. Even Easchel is too intimidated to say anything about Verge.

Verge is large and imposing with an impressive girth. In addition to utilizing abilities very likely stemming from a life exposed to the energies of the crystal monoliths, he's learned the art of traditional, mundane first aid, physiology, and even herbology. What he's never learned is so-called "bedside manner." A villager who comes to him after an accident cutting timber, for example, knows they're not only going to get healed but probably called an idiot, or worse. When his skills as a healer are not required, he's likely off doing physical labor by himself. That's probably the only time he's happy.

Thear

Sesson

Verge

NEANDRAN

Thates Fields

To Lake Memory

Gobrin Grazing

To The River Dock

To The Mill

Storehouse

Crystal Monolith

Crystal Monolith

Thates Fields

Temple

The Post

Crystal Monolith

Storehouses

1. Aryle and Amrose's House
2. Easchel's House
3. Gonnor's House
4. Illace's House
5. Sesson and Ien's House
6. Kyath and Ulam's House
7. Luttan's House
8. Mert's House
9. Messos and Thear's House
10. Rystan's House
11. Odet's House
12. Verge's House
13. Veri and Yurran's House

250 feet

76 meters

To the Infinite Abode

N

THE TEMPLE

A structure dominates the center of the village, unquestionably ancient. Although its composition resembles brass, the material is actually something different, with a surface surprisingly textured and rough. A ramp rises to a wide, open archway engraved with what might be flowering vines.

The structure itself is empty and hollow. There are no interior walls or original furnishings or devices. Most people become very aware upon entering that the temple—like the inside of an enormous metal bell—has strange acoustic qualities. In certain places, the merest whisper can be heard throughout the temple, but in other places, a shout is almost silent.

Surrounding the temple is a ring of unknown metal rising up out of the ground at an angle, like a halo that has fallen. The 5-foot-wide (1.5 m) metal ring makes a circle 68 feet (20 m) in diameter, but it is only 2 inches (5 cm) thick. About a third of the ring is below ground level, as though it flew through the air and embedded itself into the earth.

The people of Neandran have adopted the central structure to be used as their temple to Loe; thus, folk have always called the structure "The Temple." Although the assumption among the locals is that it was originally a temple in the prior worlds, there's absolutely no way of knowing if that's true.

Carpets of woven fibers dyed brilliant colors cover the floor, while banners of red, blue, and green hang on the walls. Other than a central platform of brightly painted wood, the temple holds no other furnishings.

Sesson, the priest of Loe, holds rites and ceremonies in their honor. He kindly welcomes any and all into the temple and is happy to teach the ways of his god, although he is neither forceful nor overbearing in that regard.

Loe is seen as a kind and loving god. A purely invisible spirit being, they are beyond gender or even appearance. The river in the valley is named for the god, as it can be seen as a means to spread Loe's blessings.

Loe comes from a myth brought to the valley with the first human settlers. There is no such being, and if Neandran has any special blessings, they likely come from the energies of the crystal monoliths, although they are as much a bane as a boon.

CRYSTAL MONOLITHS

Neandran has two tall monoliths of gleaming white crystal that turn a milky violet color when struck by sunlight and a much darker, deeper purple when exposed to moonlight. They are similar, but not identical, tapering toward the base as well as the top. Equidistant from the temple, the monoliths stand almost 60 feet (20 m) tall. As such, they're often used by locals as guide stones so that they know how to get back to the village when out in the woods.

It's not discussed openly—it's considered unseemly to speak of it—but everyone in Neandran knows that the monoliths have strange energies associated with them. These energies are believed (correctly) to increase the fertility of the land around the monoliths. They're also responsible for the frequent conjoined births of the gobrin, but also perhaps for those births being viable and healthy. Lastly, the energies are responsible for mutations in some of those born in the village, but more often than not, these rare mutations are beneficial rather than detrimental. Yes, there are somewhat more birth defects in the newborns of Neandran, but there are also those who can move objects with their minds or create ice in the palm of their hands.

THE HOUSES

By far, most of the buildings in the village are private homes. Each family lives together in their own house, with bigger families in bigger houses (house size is not a matter of status, but rather need). Most of the houses are round, and many have a cloth awning on posts in front of the entrance, creating more living and storage space. Houses are made of clay and wood.

Houses all have wood stoves for cooking and heating. They do not have locks on their doors.

THE THATES FIELDS

Long ago, villagers cleared sizable portions of land to farm as fields. Between growing seasons, the gobrin are allowed to occupy the fields, which both cuts down on weeds and other plants and fertilizes the ground.

THE POST

The common house for all Neandran is simply called the Post, and the stories told today say that in the earliest days of the village it was literally just a wooden post folks would gather around at the end of the day to talk and drink.

The Post is one of the larger buildings in Neandran, and the only one with a full second story. It is entirely timber built, and unlike the houses around it is rectangular in shape. Below lies a large, cool cellar used for storage of beverages (alcoholic and otherwise) and food.

The main room of the Post has a great many tables (some standing, some with chairs) and colorful banners on the walls and draped across the ceiling. Sometimes, Aryle will share a story or a song for everyone. At other times, he'll organize a community event in the Post with special decorations, music, and refreshments.

Bik (short for Bichel) runs the Post and lives in the upper floor. He's at his happiest making others happy and satisfied, and when he's happy, he sings. He serves drink and food—sometimes hot, sometimes not. The abundance of the repast provided perfectly mirrors the abundance of the village. When the stores are full, so are the bellies of those who go to the Post.

THE STOREHOUSES

All of the village's supplies, whether they be food, grain, tools, cloth, or anything else, are kept in these buildings. The doors here do not have locks.

Luttan keeps a detailed inventory of all the storehouses, and when something is running low, she will try to correct that—often ahead of time. For example, if it is approaching thates-harvesting time, she asks various skilled folks to construct some new tools if the current supply appears insufficient. And she of course provides them with the materials, probably from a different storehouse.

At any given time, the village of 400+ will have two or three folks who've been affected adversely by the monoliths, and five or six who have some special gift. The PCs who have special abilities represent those with powers from the monoliths right now, plus Illace, Verge, and Odet.

THE MILL

The mill is really just a small shack by the river, overseen by Odet. A waterwheel turns the mechanism in the building to grind thates into flour. A second small building with two open walls is used to store thates and various tools. Odet collects the ground flour, which gets taken back to the village where Luttan makes sure it gets placed safely in storage.

VILLAGE EVENTS

Once the campaign has started, Neandran does not remain static. If they are present, the PCs can participate or help, and if they are not they will hear about whatever they missed after the fact.

- Ien, Sesson's husband, grows very ill with a stomach ailment. Village treatments including those from the Old Witch don't help much. There is talk of getting him to Ketterach to see if there's something the people there can do.
- Gonnor's depression gets worse. He disappears for a few days and people go out to find him in the woods. His partner Alloise asks if someone will go to the Old Witch to see if she has a solution (she does; it's an elixir she calls Delight).
- Luttan and Navrati (Thear's son) get married. It's a large celebration in and around the temple, with a majority of the village in attendance. Aryle recites a poem that he wrote just for them, and it's funny and moving.
- A fire destroys Easchel's home. He blames sorcery and accuses people in the village he was already suspicious of as being responsible.

VILLAGE GM INTRUSIONS

If in the course of play a GM intrusion occurs in the village itself, here are some suggestions:

- A gobrin gets spooked and bolts into the woods. It will be lost if not caught or found.
- A physical action by the character causes them to inadvertently bump into a villager that they didn't even realize was there. A failed Speed defense roll (difficulty 2) means that the villager is knocked to the ground, suffers a point of damage, and is very angry.
- Kids run out to talk to the character, getting in the way of whatever they were trying to do.
- Cold rain makes anyone the character tries to talk to grumpy, hindering any interaction task.
- A fire starts in a nearby home!
- Bik's still for making thates alcohol breaks down. This makes anyone the character tries to talk to grumpy, hindering any interaction task. If a character can repair the contraption (difficulty 3), however, interaction tasks within the Post are eased for the rest of the day.

Also see Chapter 29: Guiding a Community

Narth: *level 3*

IN TIMES OF TROUBLE

Danger in Neandran typically means a sarrat has ventured too near the village for everyone's comfort, or one of the buildings catches fire. In such cases, all those able to help band together to solve the problem. In the case of a fire, everyone pitches in, although you can count on Amrose, Narth, Messos, and Luttan to be leading the effort. In the case of illness or injury, it's Verge that steps in, but Ulam, Illace, Rystan, and Sesson would help if they can. If the village has a threat that must be dealt with using violence, you can be sure that people turn to Kyath, Mert, and perhaps Messos.

Aryle, Bik, and some of the others likely don't provide much help in times of trouble, but they're good to have around afterward when people need to relax or find comfort.

The Uldada is a unique situation and covered in detail in chapter 10.

CHAPTER 4

THE VALLEY

The Glimmering Valley resembles a glaciated valley with steep sides and a mostly flat valley floor. However, there is more here than meets the eye.

The valley sides show signs of straight edges like walls, and even protuberances that might have been pipes or conduits. The valley, then, isn't the result of time eroding the earth's natural surface, but rather eroding some structure or structures from the distant past.

In places, however, the tops of the valley sides curve inward, suggesting the edges of a roof long gone. Local artists have created different interpretive art of what the valley might have looked like in ages past, but there is no consensus and of course it's all speculation anyway.

One end of the valley spills into a grassland to the southwest. To the northeast, the head of the valley eventually disappears into the mountains, with sheer rock walls that divide into a tangle of clefts and ravines, usually wet with snowmelt.

Loe's River flows through the center of the valley. It begins in the tangled end of the valley, where dramatic waterfalls and trickles from tiny hanging valleys (more like gullies) pour down into Lake Memory.

Not that anyone in the village of Neandran knows (or cares), but the Glimmering Valley is located in Thaemor in the Steadfast, just to the west of the Black Ridge. That means that its climate is temperate and the valley experiences distinct seasonal changes. More than half the trees in the heavily wooded valley are deciduous, and thus grow bare in the fall and bloom with a thick canopy of leaves in the spring.

You can, of course, put the valley wherever you want in the Ninth World.

A gentle breeze whispers through the branches. A fallen log provides home to a variety of insects and animals, as well as some orange fungus. Saplings spring forth from the damp earth beneath a carpet of fallen leaves and pine needles.

An older tree creaks, bemoaning its great age. Earthy scents mixing decay and new life intermingle in a mélange you'll find nowhere else. Mushrooms thrive in those spots that haven't seen the light of the sun since the valley formed and the trees grew like living monoliths, with an enveloping canopy so thick it's difficult to know where one tree ends and another begins. Leaves and ferns glisten with a dark, rich green that seems to radiate health. A thicket stirs with the movement of birds, hunting for seeds. Spiders' webs stretch from plant to plant across what passes for a path.

You know to cut or avoid the thorny vines wrapping around every tree, every rock, every deadfall as well as draping across the path. Those same vines burst with berries in the summer, and you grew up craving berry-stuffed thates rolls on a warm day. This is the valley. These are the woods. This is your home.

MOVING AROUND THE VALLEY

Although folks in Neandran don't use (or need) a map of the valley, one is provided for the GM in this book. Although not marked on the map, there are rougher, narrower paths—created by hunters, foragers, or wildlife, mostly—that can make crossing distances easier. Neandran natives all know how to get from the village to the river as well as to the nearby cleared fields, and almost everyone has been to Lake Memory at least a few times in their lives. Only more experienced travelers know how to get to other locations without help. There are no maps, but directions from knowledgeable people are easily garnered. Most directions are simple, such as "follow the path north and west and you'll get there." Inexperienced people just heading into the woods off the paths are absolutely certain to get lost. (As the valley walls are high and even curved inward in many places,

even using the sun for a sense of direction is only an option in the middle of the day.)

Unless an area is specifically cleared—like the village, the nearby fields, or the paths—the valley floor is twisted with growth and treacherous with tumbled rocks and fallen logs as well as surprising ruts, hollows, or animal burrows. At any given moment, assume that the ground is not flat and not clear. It's also damp. Puddles accumulating under the undergrowth and rocks and trees slick with moisture are common.

On a path, those on foot can move about 2 miles (3 km) in an hour, double that if in a real hurry. Off the paths, that same traveler will be fortunate to get half that distance, and moving in a hurry is a Speed task with a difficulty of 3. Failure probably means a twisted ankle or a banged-up knee from a trip or slip.

Physical tasks other than hiking carefully (such as fighting) probably are hindered by at least 1 step.

Map of the Glimmering Valley, page 8

The valley is filled with whatever wildlife you feel appropriate. For example, there are "turtles" and "frogs" in the river, and that is probably what the Neandrans call them, but they don't necessarily look like what we would call turtles and frogs. In other words, there's nothing wrong with telling the players they see a "squirrel" in a tree, but then—maybe— mention its long, ratlike tail or vestigial wings. Walk that line between familiar and interesting, and remember, this is a billion years in the future.

VALLEY FLORA

These are some of the more common plants that grow in the Glimmering Valley, with the names Neandrans use.

Atish: Plant that grows in bulbous pale-green bunches upon the ground. As a part of their life process, they expel jets of lighter-than-air gas straight upward. Enough of these will produce a steady stream of gas that can hold fairly light objects aloft. An entire patch of these can even keep a buat afloat.

Tyr-ana, page 118

Balla: Ubiquitous leafy green-and-yellow vines that stretch out across rocks, wrap around other plants, and stretch out along the ground, amid the tough grasses and wildflowers. The leaves are edible, but unpleasant and only moderately nutritious.

Buat: Fungal-plant hybrids that float above a patch of atish and the steady jets of gas they emit, often about 10 to 20 feet (3 to 6 m) in the air. To foster the atish, the buat rain down clouds of nutrient-rich particles that can sustain the plants below them, while the buat are in fact carnivorous and feed on insects and even small birds that get too close

Erien tree: The erien grows to be 30 or more feet (10+ m) in height. The tree's trunk is relatively narrow and often slightly curved. The leaves are few but enormous, with every branch sprouting just one each. These massive leaves are thick and sturdy, and those with some know-how use fallen leaves as shelters or even small boats.

Luva: Tall, narrow conifers with dark green needles. Their seed cones are edible.

Soldier oaks: Very likely the most common trees in the valley, these are tall, sturdy deciduous trees, as their name suggests. Their wood is excellent for building and crafting.

Tyr-ana: These extremely rare trees have crimson, leafless branches. Most notably, however, their lower trunks appear to have two humanoid legs, and they can uproot themselves and walk. Carnivorous, they feed on small mammals and birds they lure into their scented branches, covered in poisonous barbs.

Ustis: A fairly common plant. Their tiny seeds are used as a spice in food.

Zurain: Broad, tall conifers with sky-blue needles. They are generally shorter than luva.

VALLEY FAUNA

These are some of the species of wildlife that dwell in the Glimmering Valley, with the names Neandrans use.

Baroon: Colony organism sharing traits of both insects and flightless birds. Their six legs and segmented bodies make them sturdy and strong. A fourth pair of much longer extendable limbs allows them to run at great speeds in short bursts, and can be used as talons to defend themselves.

Blue voot: As small and quick as their red-plumed cousins while quieter and more subdued, these birds are clever collectors of shiny objects.

Chichachi: Named for the sound they seem to whisper, these creatures resemble enormous bioluminescent inchworms that make their way through the woods. Seeing one is considered a good omen—killing one is thought to bring disaster upon all involved.

Coppo: Silver-scaled fish are found in the lake and the river and are another source of food for Neandran.

Decsa: The swift, brilliantly plumed birds use a distinct call that sounds like a mournful wail. Because of this, they are sometimes called wailing birds or grief birds.

Harrow hawk: Nesting in the upper reaches of the valley walls, these nimble predatory birds master the skies above the valley. Some folk in Ketterach have trained these birds for hunting and even defense.

Hornhog: Small, tree-dwelling mammals, these brownish-red creatures and their high-pitched snorts are ubiquitous in the valley. As their name suggests, their heads have small horns that they use to defend themselves.

Nobba: Burrowing mammals capable of impressive bursts of speed when threatened.

Rean: Graceful bipedal herbivores known for their extreme wariness and heightened senses. Only the most skilled hunter can bring down a rean, but those that can are rewarded with a lot of highly prized meat.

Red voot: These spritely, red-feathered birds are quite intelligent, and quite temperamental. They swoop menacingly and screech if anyone gets too close to their nest.

Sarrat: These large feline predators' glands produce hallucinogenic chemicals they can spit up to an immediate distance to confuse prey and make them easier to bring down.

Veeshin: Venomous snakes that hunt in packs (or perhaps rather, swarms). Unlike many other serpents, they do not swallow prey whole. Instead, they secrete acid that breaks down the flesh of their prey so that they can easily swallow the almost-liquified remains. Known for their brilliant colors and their hissing, which many liken to a "sizzling" sound.

Baroon, page 109

Blue voot: *level 1, level 3 for Speed defense; moves a long distance in flight*

Chichachi, page 111

Rean, page 115

Red voot: *level 1, level 3 for Speed defense; moves a long distance in flight*

Coppo: *level 1, level 3 for Speed defense*

Sarrat, page 116

Decsa: *level 1, level 2 for Speed defense*

Veeshin, page 119

Harrow hawk: *level 2, level 4 for Speed defense; can move a long distance in flight*

Hornhog: *level 1, level 2 for Speed defense; inflicts 2 damage*

Nobba: *level 2, level 4 for Speed defense; moves a long distance or an immediate distance burrowing*

GM intrusion: *The soil near the river's edge gives way under a character walking along it. A failed Speed defense roll (difficulty 4) means the character falls into the water. Small river crabs get in their clothes and so not only is the character soaking wet for a few hours, but they suffer from itchy pinches that hinder their actions during that period.*

The Pods, page 55

Deepers: *level 3; Armor 1; bite damage 4*

Thalgre the Oracle: *level 3, level 5 for insight and reading people*

Safe corridor, page 301

VALLEY LOCATIONS

Other than Neandran, there are a number of interesting locations in the Glimmering Valley. (Note that both Ketterach and the Ancient Crèche get their own chapters.)

LOE'S RIVER

Named for the deity revered by many of the folk in the valley, Loe's River starts at Lake Memory and runs the valley's length and into the grasslands beyond (where it certainly has a different name from the locals of that region).

The river is slow-moving in the latter part of the year and the surface will freeze over in the winter. In the spring, however, it gushes with snowmelt from the mountains, running both fast and deep, high above the banks it keeps the rest of the year.

LAKE MEMORY

Located in the cirque at the valley's head, the cold, clear waters of this deep lake pour down from the mountains in three dramatic falls as well as numerous smaller ones. Fish in the lake are plentiful, as are indigo-colored leeches that can grow to be 6 inches (15 cm) in length. In the winter, the lake's surface freezes—people can and do walk across it in the coldest months.

A handful of people live on the shores of Lake Memory, scattered around its edges. Most fish the lake from the shore or in small boats.

The Oracle: One of the folks that lives by the lake is Thalgre, an old man in a shack at the very tip of a narrow promontory jutting from the shore. Thalgre refers to himself as "The Oracle," and many others do as well. For 3 shins (or the equivalent) he will try to divine the answer to a question by consulting an ancient device of glass and metal. He stares into a screen of swirling colors and then lays it flat, tossing a handful of fish bones on it. He tries to then provide the answer to the question.

This is all nonsense, as the machine doesn't tell the future at all (its actual purpose is unfathomable in the Ninth World). A difficulty 3 task to identify numenera reveals that. However, Thalgre is a very wise and insightful man, and he reads people well. He might be able to come up

with useful advice or insightful commentary even without supernatural aid.

Sunken Treasure: The center of the lake bottom holds the remains of what appears to be some mysterious structure. While the details cannot be made out from the shore, it can be seen on a sunny day by anyone in a boat. Reaching the lake bottom is another matter. It's well known to the locals that there's something down there, but the lake is incredibly cold and the structure too deep for anyone to just dive to it.

With help from breathing equipment found elsewhere (such as the fungal suit found with the Pods in the Ancient Crèche), and some protection from the cold, characters could check it out should they wish. Doing so almost certainly draws the attention of at least six surprisingly large and aggressive predatory fish called deepers by the lake folk.

The "structure" at the bottom of the lake is a vehicle, probably a flying vehicle, with two "cockpits" clearly not intended for human pilots. While it's far, far beyond repair, the untouched wreck holds some valuable salvage. The salvage task is only level 3, but even with light and protection from the cold, the task is hindered (hindered by 2 steps without proper protections). Successful salvaging yields:

- 11 shins
- 2 units of synthsteel (iotum)
- 10 units of parts
- A level 3 cypher in the form of two glass lenses that could easily be affixed to goggles or spectacles that ease all vision-based tasks by 2 steps
- A level 6 cypher in the form of a handheld device with wires and attachments that—when affixed to another device—ease any attempt at identifying or using it (or both) by 2 steps
- A level 4 artifact in the form of two metal and synth capsules about the size of a human head, each with a large glass plate. This is a safe corridor device.

BANDIT CAMP

Belof and Echealli are a pair of siblings that lead a small band of criminals exiled (self-exiled or driven out) from Neandran. They call themselves bandits or raiders, but in truth they're more muggers and burglars than actual raiders. Recently, they have also become, for lack of a better term, drug dealers.

The band consists of six thugs and the two siblings. While the group isn't overly bloodthirsty, they'll do whatever they feel they need to do in order to get by. Or get ahead. They steal food and most of what they need from the locals, but pickings are slim and the folk in the valley don't have very much to steal.

The camp itself is nothing more than a few moss-covered tents and a crude lean-to made of sticks, all surrounding a firepit. Trash and miscellaneous junk lies strewn everywhere. A narrow trail leads down to the riverbank.

At any given time, half the band is probably present, sleeping, talking, or drunk. If they're alerted that someone's coming, they hide, either to ambush the interlopers or to avoid them. There's little of value in the camp, so they won't hesitate to leave it behind. Each is armed with a knife or a club and they wear leather jerkins.

The Drug Scheme: A few months ago, Belof discovered a bit of special moss in the woods. Dried and powdered, the substance acts as a powerful narcotic to anyone ingesting or inhaling it. It's also highly addictive. He hoped to sell this to some of his contacts in Neandran, but only a very few were interested. Echealli suggested a devious plan to create some addicts to sell to. She bought a number of Atta's minor herbal concoctions and then secretly laced the admixtures with Belof's new drug. Now they supply the witch's creations to a young accomplice named Bedor in Neandran, who attempts to give them out or trade them cheaply with the understanding that the buyer will want more and more.

The plan is, once a few victims become addicted, they will then reveal that it's the

GM intrusion: The bandits rigged up a crude tripwire trap. If a character near the camp doesn't spot it with an Intellect defense roll (difficulty 2), they trip over the line and some old pots and pans make a loud clatter.

Atta, page 39

Belof's drug: *level 2; produces severe drowsiness and reduces Edge stats by 3 for one hour; Might defense roll to avoid addiction*

drug they need to stave off withdrawal and offer to sell them the drug for whatever the band needs—food, clothing, gear, or just a few extra shins. They also plan to threaten to reveal to others in the village that the victim is an addict should they tell anyone about their predicament. They want their addicts on a leash for the long term.

It isn't a great plan. Belof and Echealli are not criminal masterminds.

Recent Events: To make matters worse, four of the six bandits that follow them have become addicted to the drug themselves, making them unreliable and (even more) incompetent. Also, a number of them recently spied Illace's cultists in the woods performing one of their ceremonies, and the bandits became quite spooked by the experience. They don't know the cultists' identities, but they suspect that Atta is in league with them, and they fear that they may be marked or cursed by sorcery.

Belof: If Belof has garnered any reputation at all other than as a ne'er-do-well, it's because of his skills as a swordsman. He wields a blade carved from an ancient metal of some sort, his pride and joy that he calls Vev.

Known only to him, Belof has a secret box hidden in the trunk of a dead tree near the camp where he keeps his supply of the drug he makes (usually a dozen or so doses); a stash of 9 shins; a smooth, egg-like stone that is a level 4 cypher that, when squeezed tightly, boosts Might Edge by 1 for an hour; and an oddity in the form of a glass rod with a red metal ball that somehow orbits around the rod when held.

Echealli: Echealli wears a coat sewn from material that she found scavenging a few years ago. This strange cloth grows instantly rigid upon forceful impact, meaning that while the coat is light armor, it provides 2 points of Armor, not just 1. (This is effectively a level 2 artifact with no depletion.) She prefers to use the buzzer she got in Ketterach in combat, but she also carries a pair of knives.

Other bandits: *level 3; Armor 1; at any given moment, about half are level 2 for all tasks thanks to the influence of drugs and alcohol*

Illace's cultists, page 25

Belof: *level 4, level 6 with a sword, level 5 in stealth and Speed defense; inflicts 6 damage with his sword*

Echealli: *level 4; level 5 in stealth, perception, and all interactions (especially) lying; Armor 2; in melee can use her buzzer or make two attacks with a knife in each hand, each inflicting 4 damage*

ATTA'S HOUSE (THE INFINITE ABODE)

For as long as anyone can remember, "the Old Witch" has lived in a very specific house in the woods called the Infinite Abode. The fact is, the person in the role of the Old Witch has changed throughout the generations, and while some might be somewhat aware of that—or at least suspect it—no one really gives it much thought. They just think of the Old Witch who brews potions and elixirs in the Infinite Abode.

The Infinite Abode is the name of a prior-worlds structure that looks, on the outside, like a series of spherical or semi-spherical shells of some unknown organic substance. To be forthright, it looks like a meringue or perhaps a pie crust. It is neither, of course, and the material is extremely sturdy and solid. It repels dirt and water and the mosses and molds that grow over most other things in the woods.

Through the wooden door set into one of the spheres, one enters a homey dwelling, complete with a fireplace, old but comfortable wooden furniture, some woven rugs, and so on. The not-quite-identifiable odor of a cooking dish permeates the place. A door of this round, domed room leads into another. And through there, another. And another. The interior of this structure appears to be infinite.

THE BANDIT THREAT

The self-styled bandits are not really intended to be a serious threat, but the players don't know that. These are the worst of the worst from Neandran, but all that really means is that even the ruffians in village are pretty much simple folk. These are really the individuals that were too lazy or stupid to be farmers or skilled workers of any kind. Belof and Echealli themselves might be a challenge for a small group of PCs, but their gang is poorly equipped and incompetent. Most are drunk or stoned, and a couple of them are quite old. Not a one of them fights to the death, and all of them are quickly demoralized. They talk a good talk, but if given any real resistance, they flee.

The various rooms, all seemingly within the organic spheres, are mostly empty. The original purpose of the structure is aeons gone, but it probably wasn't intended to be a dwelling. Given its appearance, it may be the remains of a creature or plant of some kind, grown rather than built.

The Old Witch: Atta is practically always present in the Infinite Abode. She only uses a few of the spaces within, and in fact, avoids exploring the endless succession of rooms. She's heard strange noises coming from a far distance in the house and has no interest in learning what made them.

Atta, as has been stated, is only the latest person to take on the role of "the Old Witch." Growing up in Neandran, she went by a different name and presented as male. She left the village one day to see if the Old Witch of the woods had some magic that could help transition her physically into her preferred form. When she arrived at the Infinite Abode, however, she found the occupant had passed away. The witch had left behind numerous books of her own notes about the numenera, as well as her tools and ingredients. Atta studied and practiced, teaching herself the art of potions, poultices, and elixirs.

The folk of the valley didn't seem to notice or care that the identity of the Old Witch changed, as it had at least six times before. (In the past, successors had sometimes apprenticed with the previous witch, but in one case had supplanted the role through foul play.) This isn't too surprising, as the people give the Infinite Abode and its occupant a wide berth, coming only to barter for some of her creations, and never staying long.

Atta has been the Old Witch for more than a decade and she enjoys the role, and in particular the seclusion. She is constantly trying to learn more through study and experimentation. To her, the numenera is unquestionably sorcery, and its powers come from spirits that inhabit the world, represented by the ingredients she uses.

Atta maintains an aura of mystery and even a bit of sinister intent, but this is just for show, and to keep away thieves. Those that know of the existence of Illace's demon cult may very well suspect that Atta is involved, and while she won't ever claim to be, she doesn't do much to disabuse anyone of the notion.

She knows about Illace and her followers. In fact, she makes the stealth-enhancing

Atta, the Old Witch: *level 4, level 6 for crafting numenera (and other medicines and elixirs); has a level 4 cypher in the form of a ring that can teleport her up to a very long distance*

Atta may, at some point, ask trusted acquaintances to investigate the strange noises in her house. Deep, deep within the infinite recesses of the structure, the PCs might encounter a travonis ul that will attack savagely. Slaying this ultraterrestrial beast would be something Atta would reward greatly, such as with a number of potions.

Travonis ul, page 257

Illace, page 25

Buat, page 34

Dreaming Cubes, page 42
Chichachi, page 111

Rystan, page 27

Kraat: level 4, level 5
for perception, level 1
for doing anything that
requires fine motor skills;
Armor 1; health 24; can
move in and out of phase
with the world as an
action; can attack two
adjacent foes at once
with its bashing/slicing
limbs, inflicting 4 points
of damage, or one foe
for 5 points of damage

GM intrusion: Atta takes
offense at something
unexpected. If the
character doesn't smooth
things over immediately
(difficulty 4), all
interactions between that
character and Atta are
hindered henceforth.

Luva, page 34
Voot, page 35
Baroon, page 109

concoction for them. But in truth she's afraid of them. She doesn't know if the beings in the Dreaming Cubes really can be freed, but she's terrified of the prospect. Too terrified, in fact, to say no to Illace.

She doesn't know about either the Ancient Crèche or the chambers beneath the Haunted Stair, but she has books full of old notes from previous Old Witches, and could learn a little about both if she cared to (or was somehow incentivized to). She also doesn't know anything about the Uldada or the meaning of the dream, and her notes contain nothing on either one.

Kraat: If Atta is in any danger, an automaton of sticks, broken farm tools, and bits and pieces of metal and synth charges up, seemingly from nowhere, and defends her. This is Kraat, and it obeys all her commands. It has the ability to move out of phase and follows her in this state, able to intercept any attack or threat leveled against her. Although it moves about on four limbs, it can stand up like a human as well, with a height of about 6 feet (2m). It cannot manipulate small objects, as it has little coordination of that sort and no fingers to speak of.

Atta made Kraat using secrets found in the previous Old Witch's notes. If asked, she'll say that it's powered by a soul that a devil gave her in a deal she made, but that's nonsense. It's actually a manipulation of nanotechnology.

Teaching: Atta's not keen on taking on an apprentice or teaching anyone her skills and methods. Convincing her to do so would be a difficulty 6 task. A student would be expected to live with her in the Infinite Abode and do a lot of manual labor as well as study for at least a month.

Ingredients: What Atta really cares about is to have a steady stream of ingredients so she can brew her creations. In fact, ingredients are what she prefers as payment for her wares, so that she never has to go out and gather or find them herself. Things she is interested in include:

- Grey nut shells (easy to find and gather)
- Tavithom leaves (easy to find and gather)
- Luva cones (easy to find and gather)
- Voot eggs (easy to find and gather)
- Baroon droppings (moderately difficult to find and gather)
- Buat pods (moderately difficult to find and gather)
- Chichachi organs (very difficult to find and obtain)
- Glass vials (must be obtained from the village; Rystan is a glassblower)

She speaks of most of these ingredients as mystical in nature, when in fact in her work she's just extracting valuable chemicals. Regardless, she often asks visitors to gather some of those ingredients in exchange for a potion or other creation. The first four listed could be gathered in an afternoon without any die rolls, and have a value (to Atta) of 4 shins.

The next two require special circumstances (baroon are feisty, and buat float in the air) and are difficult to locate. It might take two or even three days to procure them in the right amount, and there are probably tasks involved requiring dice rolls. These both have a value (to Atta) of about 10 shins.

Chichachi are very rare, and killing one is considered taboo. The organs' value to Atta is beyond measure. She would likely give characters one or two potions and elixirs for free whenever they stopped by, for life.

There are likely other ingredients she needs from time to time, and she can make use of iotum that could be found in places like the Ancient Crèche, although she doesn't ever ask for such things.

Potions and More: Atta makes potions, poisons, elixirs, and poultices. In her parlance, "potions" are actual cyphers. Each has a value of about 10 shins. Common potions she makes include:

- Level 4 Vitality Potion: restores 4 Might
- Level 4 Remedy: cures one disease
- Level 4 Potion of Shadow and Silence: eases stealth actions for 10 minutes
- Level 3 Potion of Tireless Speed: grants 1 Speed Edge for 1 hour
- Level 3 Potion of the Fish: drinker can breathe water for 1 hour
- Level 3 Potion of Ancient Skill: eases any numenera-related tasks for 1 hour
- Level 3 Potion of the Rean: eases any perception-related tasks for 1 hour
- Level 2 Potion of Sleep: drinker falls into a very heavy sleep for 10 minutes

- Level 2 Complacency Poison: can be injected or ingested; target is lethargic and hindered by 2 steps for an hour
- Level 2 Paralysis Poison: can be injected or ingested; complete paralysis lasts for 2 rounds; target is hindered by 2 steps for a minute afterward

Elixirs and poultices are not cyphers, but she takes them just as seriously, and so do her customers. Some are useless, but some actually have minor effects. All of these have a value of 4 shins. These concoctions include:

- Poultice of Ease: supposedly takes away chronic pain. A placebo at best.
- Elixir of Love: supposedly makes you more lovable in the eyes of someone you love. It's nonsense.
- Elixir of Luck: supposedly gives you good luck all day. It's nonsense.
- The Respite: allows you to make an immediate one-action recovery roll that doesn't count toward your limit.
- The Blue Magic: allows you to recover from an illness a day or two faster.
- Elixir of Life: prevents heart attack and stroke. Somewhat effective.
- Frogcatcher: allows you to see in dim light as though it were bright light.
- Delight: gives a mild euphoria, or alleviates depression if taken once each week.
- Clear Eye: alleviates the effects of a sarrat's spittle as well as other (non-permanent) mind-altering effects.

Lastly, Atta makes seasoning and herbal mixtures for food and drinks, cosmetics and perfumes, ointments, and dyes, as well as various sorts of cigarettes. These are all just 1 shin for a bottle or a smoke.

Atta's Keyrod: Atta's predecessor accepted a strange blue metal-and-crystal wand about 5 inches (15 cm) long as a payment for a few potions from an explorer decades ago. Atta still has it, and suspects it has some connection to the Haunted Stair, the River Ring, or some other ancient locale, but she's never investigated. It of course would be extremely valuable for investigating the stair or the Ancient Crèche. She would trade it to an interested person for something of the value of about 10 shins.

THE RIVER RING

Near the river-bank, the shell of a prior-world machine juts up from the ground, more than half buried. It has long since been stripped of anything salvageable, giving it the appearance of a corroded metal skeleton.

A nearby pond has a far more interesting and strange feature called the River Ring by the locals. While the pond is shallow and small, the water in the middle of it flows up into the air, forming a pillar about 5 feet (1.5 m) high and 3 feet (1 m) wide. At the top of this pillar, the water splits its flow and runs about 5 feet (1.5 m) in two opposite directions. Finally, the water in each flow then angles upward and toward its opposite counterpart, flowing about 10 feet (3 m) until they meet, forming a triangle of water suspended in midair.

Why is it called, by the locals, the River Ring? While not an ancient mystery like the formation itself, no one alive knows the origin of the name for certain, but most assume that in generations past, the water formed a circle rather than a triangle.

When the river is at its lowest levels, the pond all but dries up and the pillar and formation disappear with it. If this phenomenon has anything to do with the old machine nearby, no one's been able to discern the connection.

About one in three people that come near the River Ring feel a notable tingling sensation across their skin, and often their hair stands on end. There's no explanation for this.

There isn't anything more to the River Ring than presented, but if the GM wants, the formation could become a portal, or serve some other function if someone applies their knowledge of the numenera correctly. As presented, though, the point of the formation isn't to provide immediate adventure potential but rather to reinforce the omnipresent influence of the prior worlds on the setting. It is flavor—mystery and strangeness.

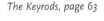

The Keyrods, page 63

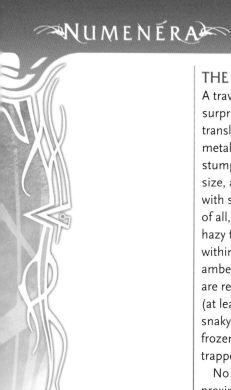

THE DREAMING CUBES

A traveler entering this glade may be surprised to find a series of enormous translucent blue cubes resting atop glistening metal pedestals which almost resemble tree stumps. While the cubes are not uniform in size, all are at least 6 feet (2 m) to a side, with some closer to twice that. Strangest of all, however, is that if one gets close, the hazy form of a living creature can be seen within each cube, like a fly suspended in amber. Each creature is different, and none are recognizable as a creature alive today (at least in this region). Long, gangly limbs, snaky bodies, frills, tendrils, and more are frozen as if the creature was somehow trapped while in motion.

No grass or other plants grow in close proximity to the cubes or their pedestals. No animals willingly enter the barren glade at all.

Locals tell legends that the creatures inside are demons, trapped by a powerful god (some say Loe, others may claim differently) for their crimes, cursed to forever sleep within the cubes.

Some believe in both the reality and the power of the demons within the cubes. Illace in Neandran teaches that these beings can grant blessings to those that pay them homage, and if the demons, which she calls the Uttarek, could be freed, their faithful worshippers would be elevated to the ranks of immortals themselves. She leads the small cult that sneaks out of the village at least once a month to perform rituals here.

Even a casual passerby might spot signs of recent activity. A half-burned candle stub here, or a torn piece of cloth there. A careful search reveals that one of the cubes bears bloody handprints. These are all remnants of the cult's ritual activities.

There is an artifact known as the Lost Cube that can perhaps free the beings in the cubes.

Lost Cube, page 47

THE EMPTY CAVES

Not truly caves at all, this subterranean complex exists within the valley wall—and the valley walls are actually ancient structures. Access to a portion of the interior of one of these structures looks like an overgrown cave mouth, but once the viny curtain is pulled away, ancient metal and synth interiors quickly reveal the true nature of these "caves."

The people of the valley have known about these chambers for a long time, and likely plundered them for useful technologies or oddities in the distant past. Today, while the caves are still regarded as dangerous and possibly haunted, no one really expects to find treasures or secrets within. More likely one will stumble upon a sarrat lair or a nest of veeshin.

Any salvage attempted here yields only parts.

LAIR OF THE TOOTHED EYE

What has appeared for aeons as a tree-covered hill actually houses a biomechanical being from the prior worlds. This thing has been seen in the dream shared by all in the valley since people first came here, and it has become known as the toothed eye. During Stage Two of the Uldada, a door in this hill opens and the inhabitant exits, attempting to locate the structure being built.

This means that should the PCs come upon this locale, they won't find the creature, but the empty lair. Conversely, they may encounter the creature simply roaming about the valley.

The lair is a synth geodesic dome (covered over with millennia of soil and plants). The interior is entirely a color not normally found in nature, but seen in the dream: *vell*. *Vell* is closer to orange and yellow than it is to blue and red, but it really is something you can't fully describe if you've never seen it. It's jarring and off-putting to most people, even if they've had the dream.

The interior is filled with ancient mechanisms and interconnected devices.

A successful task to search with a difficulty of 4 conducted in the lair means that the characters find a level 5

fireproofing spray cypher and a level 7 repair sphere artifact, both stored in what seems to be some kind of synth receptacle (kind of like a sealed cabinet). However, there are protective measures defending the receptacle. Should anyone open it without tapping out a complex code on the door—which the PCs have no way of knowing—all within the lair must succeed at Intellect defense rolls (difficulty 5) or become argumentative and irritable.

Salvage: Salvaging the interior of the dome provides even more treasures, if successful. It is a difficulty 8 task. The following can be gained/assembled:

- A level 5 cypher in the form of an air-powered projectile that could easily be mounted on a person's wrist with a strip of leather. The projectile flies up to a very long range and unleashes a pulse of energy in an immediate area. Anyone in the area is affixed to anything they are touching (handheld object, the ground, their clothing, etc.) for 10 minutes.
- A level 4 cypher in the form of a pair of metal cylinders about 10 inches (25 cm) in length. After being activated, each has a small readout that displays the direction and distance to the other cylinder for the next 28 hours.
- A level 8 cypher in the form of a metallic disk that produces a personal force field around the user, granting +2 Armor for one hour.
- An oddity that is a trio of synth balls that cannot be made to touch. They can only get get about 1 inch (2.5 cm) apart before they exert inexorable force holding each other at bay.
- 8 io
- 4 units of bio-circuitry (iotum)
- 4 units of azure steel (iotum)
- 40 units of parts
- 2 shins

Fireproofing spray, page 279

Repair sphere, page 300

GM intrusion: *A victim of the emotion-changing trap actually attacks one of the other characters in anger.*

In the dome, the GM can allow PCs to attempt two salvaging tasks, each with a difficulty of 5, rather than the one task at difficulty 8. However, in such a case, the first successful task salvages only the level 4 and 5 cyphers and the oddity, and the other task results in half of the listed iotum, parts, and shins, if successful.

Uldada, page 93

Toothed Eye, page 117

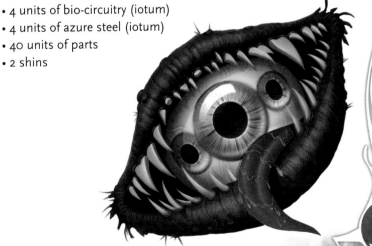

CHAPTER 5

VALLEY ENCOUNTERS

Ardiss: *level 3, level 6 when interacting with or using advanced machines; Armor 1; can sense advanced machines if they have power and lie within short range; has two level 3 cyphers—a crystal wand that restores 3 points of Might and a handheld device that provides an energy field giving +1 Armor for one hour*

Explorer's pack, page 98

There will be a lot of travel in a Glimmering Valley campaign, almost entirely traipsing along paths through the forest. The point of these encounters is to show the dynamic nature of the stories in the valley, not to punish the PCs for traveling a lot. In general, no more than one encounter a day is probably appropriate, and it really depends on the pacing of the game session.

For the most part, these encounters may happen anywhere in the valley, at any time, although a few work better in certain portions of the valley and at different times. These are noted in their description.

Some of the encounters should happen only once, while others can and should happen multiple times. You can choose which encounter you want, or you can roll randomly.

ARDISS

Ardiss comes from Ketterach, and he is exploring the valley on his own. Specifically, he's interested in uncovering some of the prior-world tech that might be found in the woods. He has an average build and chiseled features, but is remarkably short. He wears a leather jerkin adorned with bits of metal and synth he's taken from ancient devices (about 12 shins) and carries a knife as well as an explorer's pack.

He is a technopath and can mentally communicate with and sometimes control advanced machines. He has no idea where this ability comes from. He shrugs if asked. "Machines just have always talked to me, ever since I was a boy."

If the PCs are friendly and are also exploring or just traveling the same way he's going, Ardiss would be pleased to

Encounter	Die Roll	Frequency	Narrative Driver
Ardiss	01–05	Once	None
A Bit of Weird	06–10	Once	None
Briinii Lost	11–20	Once	Cannot happen until briinii arrive
Chichachi	21–23	Once	None (after sunset)
Criminals and Ruffians	24–30	Once (perhaps twice)	None
Glimmer	31–44	Multiple	None (but should happen)
Hunting Sarrata	45–49	Once	None
Lost Cube	50–55	Once	None
Mert	56–59	Once	None
Mist	60–66	Multiple	None
Nyka on the Trail	67–70	Once	Should happen after Essatha takes notice of the PCs
Ourach Scouts	71–75	Once	Should happen after ourach invade
The Screaming Spirit	76–85	Once	None (after sunset)
Snow	86–90	Multiple	None
The Toothed Eye	91–94	Multiple	Happens after the Uldada's Stage Two
The Trader	95–00	Multiple	None

join them, at least for a while. If they're not interested, he will shrug and bid them safe journeys. He shows an interest in any cyphers or other devices they might have and can help identify or repair them if needed. He's an honest person and has no desire to steal anything (although he might trade for what he has if they have something really interesting).

The Discovery: At some point in their shared journey, Ardiss will stop. "I hear something whispering." None of the PCs are likely to hear anything if they try. Ardiss will insist that he hears something, and heads into the thickest part of the nearby woods. The going is slow, but if the PCs go with him, with their help he will uncover a 6-foot (2 m) metal dome covered by dirt and plants. In fact, the roots of a tree have encircled half of the dome as the tree grew up around it.

Getting into the dome requires one of the following:

- About ten hours of digging into the soil and cutting through roots to reveal the dome-topped cylinder. The diggers can find a sort of hatch on the side that can be forced open (level 3 task).
- Something able to pierce the level 8 metal.
- A difficulty 4 numenera knowledge-based task that reveals a removable panel behind which are exposed mechanisms that can be used to cause the dome to shudder and rise and reveal itself to be a dome-topped cylinder. It stops with a groan of finality. Essentially, this structure was once mobile, and freeing itself from the ground took the last ergs of power that it possessed.

Even after access is gained, however, danger remains. Inserting anything into the interior of the machine sets off a device that produces weird radiation visible as a pink flare of light. Anyone within immediate distance of the dome when this happens who fails a Might defense task (difficulty 5) suffers 5 points of damage and moves 1 step down the damage track. This will keep happening unless it is deactivated (difficulty 5 task, or Ardiss can do it automatically with his technopathy now that this device is active).

Inside, this machine (probably some kind of large flying drone) offers valuable salvage. Success (difficulty 5) yields:

- A level 5 cypher in the form of a short metal cylinder that instantly filters contaminants from the air in a medium area and continues to do so for 28 hours
- A level 6 cypher in the form of a long staff-like metal rod with controls at one end that emits a grey ray of energy that only affects inorganic materials, and inflicts 6 points of damage
- An oddity that is a tiny metal bit about the size of a thumb with three legs. If placed on a solid surface it scampers about on its own until it is picked up again.
- 4 units of apt clay (iotum)
- 10 units of io
- 10 units of parts
- 12 shins

Further Adventures: If invited, and if the prospect of discovering more numenera caches looks good, Ardiss will continue with the PCs on their adventures, as long as he's well-treated and welcome.

A BIT OF WEIRD

No trek across any expanse of the Ninth World would be complete without the inexplicable. The PCs make their way toward a location in the valley when the leaves and twigs and dirt on the ground immediately in front of them begin to swirl into the air. The spot crackles and sparks, and suddenly appearing on the ground is a small lumpy creature that looks a little like a cross between a frog and a starfish, with five limbs radiating from the center. The creature is completely harmless, and scuttles away if approached.

Characters that search that spot on the ground find an oval of *vell*-colored metal buried about an inch below the dirt, leaves, and needles. The oval is about 8 inches long and might serve as an oddity for trading purposes due to its color, although it never does anything out of the ordinary if removed.

BRIINII LOST

Briinii, page 91

Iea: (pronounced Aye-ee-ah) level 2, level 3 with all tasks related to the numenera

Belof and Echealli, page 37

Bedor, page 24

Once the biomechanical humanoid nomads known as the briinii are in the valley (probably a few weeks after the campaign begins), a relatively young briinii named Iea becomes lost. They hide when they see or hear the PCs coming, but not very well. The PC with the most careful eye spots them in the brush. Iea has never spoken to humans before, and they are a little surprised that they speak the same language, more or less.

Leery at first, Iea warms to friendly humans quite quickly. They would appreciate a little food and water, but they're not in dire need.

Iea knows about the "strange cave" that leads into the Ancient Crèche, although they don't know that name. In fact, that's how they got lost—they were looking for the cave that the others of their people were talking about. The young briinii heard it was filled with "ancient things" and they wanted to see them, whatever they were.

Returning Iea to the briinii camp will go a long way toward establishing a positive relationship with the clan. On the other hand, Iea might be able to lead the PCs to the strange cave, if they don't return to the briinii camp right away.

CHICHACHI

Chichachi, page 111

This encounter works best at dusk or at night, because the PCs will see a glow in the woods before they see anything else. A phosphorescent, massive inchworm-like chichachi makes its way through the dark, misty woods, its eerie light making no secret of where it is. If the PCs don't disturb it in any way, they spot another in the distance, and another.

The people of the valley consider this to be a very good omen. If any of the characters fervently believes this, allow them to have an asset on a single upcoming task of some importance—not because the legends about the chichachi are true, but because of the placebo effect and the overall positive feeling the character has.

CRIMINALS AND RUFFIANS

Not everyone in the valley is a friend.

If the PCs have not encountered Belof and Echealli or their "bandits," this encounter could take place near Neandran, with a few of the thugs headed into the village to meet up with Bedor.

If the PCs have already encountered the ruffians in their camp or are considerably farther away from the village and closer to Ketterach, they might encounter a far more serious danger in the form of some hardened criminals that truly deserve the label "bandit."

These people are not from Neandran, but Ketterach (although they're not welcome in that city and live out in the woods). They waylay travelers and traders. They know of Neandran and refer to the people from there unkindly as "forest folk" or "tree people."

Sark: level 6, level 7 for stealth and Speed defense; Armor 2; health 25

Sark's bandits: level 3, level 4 for stealth; Armor 1

Six of them wait along the path, ready to ambush the PCs. As they are trained in stealth, the difficulty to spot the ambush is 4. They demand all the travelers' valuables and food, or threaten to kill all of them. If they refuse, Sark, leader of the bandits, attempts to make an example out of one of the PCs with a shockingly fast and ruthless attack and then claims that everyone will face the same. If a fight breaks out, the PCs (being PCs) will likely all attack Sark, thinking that if they disable the leader the rest will surrender, but Sark is very difficult to hurt. Ironically, a better way to end the fight quickly would be to take out one or two of the bandits, which will make everyone flee (no one wants to die for whatever meager possessions the PCs probably have).

They are all armed with crossbows and swords, and wear leather jerkins. Sark himself wears chainmail. He also has a level 6 cypher in the form of an injector that restores 6 points of Might (or in his case, 6 points of health).

Sark and his bandits always have an escape route planned should things go poorly. In this case, it's a disguised, overgrown path that forks in two directions. The circumstances allow the bandits to use stealth and attempt to move away while hidden to elude the PCs if they pursue.

GLIMMER

There is a discussion of glimmers in Chapter 1: For the GM, but it's worth reiterating here: the PCs should be experiencing glimmers in the valley. The *Glimmering* Valley. Many will be meaningless, but some should be useful. Sometimes the PCs should find a spot where glimmers happen more often, like a signal is being transmitted to that spot.

HUNTING SARRATA

A rean dashes across the path in front of the PCs. Those who think to glance to where it came from (as opposed to where it is going) see a hunting pair of sarrata bounding toward them. These predators are happy to switch to different (and slower) prey in the form of a few people caught by surprise.

Someone with knowledge of the creatures of the valley may know (difficulty 3) that sarrata actually hunt in trios, not in pairs, and they'll know to expect a third hunter. And sure enough, the third appears, coming from a flanking position and attacking with surprise (unless someone knows to expect it).

LOST CUBE

The leafless upper branches of an otherwise normal-looking tree appear to swaddle a cube, about four feet (1 m) across. It looks very much like one of the Dreaming Cubes; however, unlike those, its corners and edges are worn, and cracks show in its surface.

The Cube: The cube is approximately 18 feet (6 m) above the ground. Only if someone gets up close to it will they be able to determine if there is a shadowy presence within, like in the actual Dreaming Cubes.

There is not. Instead, should someone get that close, something deep within the smokey, translucent cube begins to glow with an orange light. If someone then touches the cube, they find its surface to be pleasantly warm. Suddenly, and without warning, the light disappears, the cube turns granite grey, and an odd device appears in the person's hand.

The cube henceforth is inert, and in fact, crumbles to dust over the coming weeks.

The Device: The device seems to be made of solid, heavy glass and looks like a short rod with a rounded pyramid on either end. Each side of each pyramid is a slightly different color if held to the light.

This device is more or less a key for the Dreaming Cubes. Bringing it into the vicinity of the cubes causes it to vibrate slightly and glow. The shadowy shapes within the cubes begin to move and squirm, as if violently awakened. If touched to a cube, the device ceases to glow everywhere other than one of the pyramid sides. The shadowy figure within the cube is gone.

The Cult of the Uttarek: Illace has been praying that a key would manifest itself to her to allow the Uttarek to escape their prisons. Is the lost cube the answer to her prayers? She would certainly think so.

MERT

You remember Mert, the hunter from Neandran. She's had some luck over the last couple of days, both good and bad. "Sure could use a hand or two to help get this back to the village," she says, revealing three hefty burlap sacks, and the fresh corpse of a rean. Further, Mert's wounded, having run afoul of a sarrat.

Two of the sacks are full of game meat she's already field dressed and wrapped, and another is full of some hides and pelts. Not only is it a heavy load, but it needs to get back before it spoils. Mert's injury makes it impossible to get back to the village in time without help.

If the PCs help, Mert does two things:
1. She tells everyone in the village who will listen how wonderful the PCs are.
2. She gives the PCs a bag of baroon droppings. She assures them that if they take that sack to the Old Witch, she'll be quite grateful (it's worth a potion in exchange to Atta).

Glimmers, page 12

Rean, page 115

Sarrat, page 116

Mert, page 27

The lost cube encounter should occur well away from the Dreaming Cubes, and narratively probably works best if it happens after the PCs have visited the Dreaming Cubes.

The Old Witch, page 39

Nyka, page 107

Chapter 12: Essatha, page 104

The screaming spirit: *level 6; immune to physical attacks, but cannot inflict physical damage; scream inflicts 3 Intellect damage (ignores Armor) on all within long range who fail an Intellect defense roll to resist and further hinders all actions of those who hear it within short range for 3 rounds*

The screaming spirit's scream effects are cumulative, so if a creature within short distance fails their defense roll on 2 consecutive rounds, their actions are hindered by 2 steps. Keep track of rounds and penalties carefully.

Ourach, page 100

MIST

When mist rolls into the valley, it is serious. The mist is dense and it lingers for hours or even across multiple days. Characters in the mist can only see for about 10 feet (3 m) around them (an immediate area) and melee attacks (and similar physical actions requiring sight) are hindered. Ranged attacks beyond immediate range are impossible.

NYKA ON THE TRAIL

A figure with extensive prosthetics and mech parts comes down the trail. This is Nyka, and they seem friendly—a little relieved, in fact, to encounter friendly folk in the woods. They say that they are looking for something, and ask if the PCs have any information.

Nyka's a liar. They work for Essatha and were sent to intercept the PCs. What Nyka claims to be looking for depends on what the PCs did to attract Essatha's attention:

- If they have entered the Ancient Crèche, Nyka's looking for it. "An old cave in the cliff wall . . . but it's maybe not *just* a cave."
- If they entered the chambers beneath the Haunted Stair, then that's what Nyka's searching for. "A staircase in the middle of the woods that goes up to nothing."
- Otherwise, Nyka claims to be looking for "a nice little village" that they heard about. "I heard the people there are friendly, and I'm looking to see if there are any trading opportunities."

Nyka's real goal is to get an idea of who the PCs are, what they know, and what they're capable of. To do this, they spend as much time with the PCs as possible. If they can manage it, Nyka would like to accompany them, altering their story so that it seems as though they're headed to the same place as the PCs are.

OURACH SCOUTS

Four ourachs, one riding a cormental with a corenda beneath it, are making their way through the woods. These are deep advance scouts, attempting to find any other locations in the valley worth conquering. It's likely very important to Neandran that these scouts are slain, driven off, or lured away from the village because little Neandran isn't so small that the horde won't take the time to attack. What's more, they'd likely burn the forest as well.

The scouts are watchful, but nevertheless not terribly hard to ambush if the PCs decide to. If this is the characters' first experience with ourach (which is likely), observing these scouts for a while reveals their true nature. While the PCs watch, they stop to capture and torment some forest animal (drawing out its fear) before killing it. They are abusive to their own companions and disdainful of the woods in general.

THE SCREAMING SPIRIT

Legends in Neandran speak of a ghostly apparition that can be seen making its way through the woods in the valley, floating well above the ground but below the canopy above. Supposedly, they say, if it sees you, it screams so loudly and shrilly that you can't stand the sound.

The legends are true, although the "spirit" is no ghost in any mythical sense. Rather it is an ultraterrestrial being left behind from the prior worlds. Utterly solitary, it wanders the valley angry and confused.

Ideally, this encounter occurs at night, while it's raining (or possibly snowing, depending on the time of year). The PCs see a blue-green phosphorescent glow in the distance. If they investigate, it quickly becomes clear that the glow comes from a humanoid being floating well above the ground. Before the PCs can act, the ghostly figure screams, and it continues to scream until the PCs flee (or until they are dead, but it really only wants to drive them away).

It can only be harmed by energy attacks or those useful against incorporeal targets, but should the spirit suffer any damage at all, it flees. If the PCs follow it, they find it in a sodden gully near the riverbank, where a crystal the size of a person juts up out of the mud.

The crystal isn't something the PCs can salvage, but it has a strange effect upon anyone touching it. The character has their Intellect pool fully restored and they gain a +1 to their Intellect edge for the next 28 hours. This effect only happens once.

SNOW

If it's at least a few weeks into the campaign (or any time thereafter), it snows. Snow makes traveling somewhat more difficult, but it's much easier to follow tracks. Once it snows once or twice in the valley, it's likely cold enough that some of the animal life, such as baroon and hornhogs, grows scarce (nestled in their winter burrows for most of the day and night).

A heavy snowfall can slow travel dramatically, from doubling the time it takes to get somewhere to making it impossible. Seasoned woods folk all have a story or two about being trapped in the forest, away from the village, for a few days because of the snow.

Consecutive heavy snowstorms could cut Neandran off from the valley for weeks, but that's probably not a good turn for the campaign.

THE TOOTHED EYE

If the Uldada has reached Stage Two, the toothed eye is loosed and searching the woods. It's terrifying to finally encounter in reality the monstrosity that the characters have seen in their dreams every night. In fact, seeing it for the first time forces characters from Neandran to succeed at an Intellect defense roll (difficulty 6). Failure means that they are so afraid that all their actions are hindered until they are demonstrably safe from the creature.

The toothed eye has no interest in the PCs, and should they leave it undisturbed, it ignores them. It is clearly searching for something (the Uldada) and the characters might guess (correctly) that it means bad things for the village.

THE TRADER

A woman wearing a long coat, a three-pointed hat, and a backpack is walking the path. Behind her comes another person, tall and muscular, with an even larger backpack. The woman is Odyssa, and she is a trader from Ketterach. It's possible the PCs have seen her come to Neandran before.

Her hired porter is Tuwa, and they don't ever say anything. Odyssa is quite eloquent, however—a consummate salesperson. She's interested in shins but even more in what seem like prosperous trades—rare materials, cyphers, oddities, and iotum.

If coming from Ketterach, she and Tuwa carry some jars of flavorful and spicy sauces and jams unavailable in Neandran, each worth about 2 shins. She's also got a variety of metal utensils and tools.

If coming from Neandran, they carry ground thates flour, gobrin milk, and a variety of dried meats. If the PCs haven't been back home in a while, she might have news.

In either case, she's got a variety of cyphers and oddities, as well as about 20 units of parts.

Cyphers: Although her stock is always changing, she could have cyphers such as:
- A level 3 injector that cures any disease of level 3 or lower
- A level 4 canister that sprays a liquid that permanently makes a nonliving object about the size of a person float 20 feet (6 m) in the air if left alone and weightless if carried
- A level 2 injector that sustains and nourishes a creature the size of a person or a bit larger for 10 days

Oddities: Although her stock is always changing, she could have such oddities as:
- A glass cube that is as soft as a pillow
- Two metal and glass orbs that are freezing cold when apart, but heat to approximately body temperature when in contact with each other
- Razor-sharp piece of metal that only cuts inorganic materials

Taking Orders: If there is something specific that the PCs request, Odyssa will look for it when she returns to Ketterach. There's a decent chance that she'll return to Neandran with the request filled within three weeks. But the PCs better offer something really good in trade.

Tuwa: level 3, level 4 for any task related to strength or endurance; health 18; Armor 1

Food, page 23
Domesticated animals, page 23

Uldada, page 93
Lair of the Toothed Eye, page 43
Toothed Eye, page 117

Odyssa: level 4, level 6 for persuasion and trading

CHAPTER 6

THE HAUNTED STAIR

The Keyrods, page 63

In the individual room descriptions for the chapter, in addition to the description of the area, you will find important information listed succinctly in bullet point form for easy, quick reference.

Mybren: *level 5, level 3 for local knowledge, level 6 for numenera tasks and Speed defense; has an artifact that sends him to a pocket dimension for a minute if he's about to suffer damage*

In his bag, Mybren has a variety of synth tools, about 100 feet (30 m) of synth rope, a jar of 30 pills (each sustains a person for one day in terms of food and water), and some extra clothing

Essatha (page 104) has placed a camera pointed at the Haunted Stair. Only someone actively searching could find it and even then, it is a difficulty 6 task.

Uldada, page 93

Gonnor or Mert may have shared this location with the PCs back in Neandran.

Hatch: *level 8*

Difficult to find, overgrown and concealed by trees, a staircase stands alone in the woods. Made of synth and metal, these steep stairs are obviously ancient, and they just simply end after thirteen steps, about 12 feet (4 m) above the ground. It also appears that some lower portion of the staircase is buried in the ground—it's unknown how far down they go, or if they connect to anything. The trees have literally grown up around the stairs, and branches have woven themselves around the steps.

Not far from the stairs—perhaps thirty paces or so away—a synth pole about 12 feet (4 m) high rises from the ground amid the foliage. The pole would likely have been lost in the woods forever, were it not topped by a large yellow crystal that glows with a light bright enough at night to read by if one stood at the base of the pole.

Local legends in Neandran sometimes involve the stairs, although in truth very few people have ever actually seen them. The stories involve ghosts that ascend and descend the ancient staircase, or they describe some mystical land of ghosts and demons that can be found by climbing up during a full moon.

None of these stories are true. But the staircase is real. Should anyone actually excavate the lower portion, they find that there are six more steps, more than 5 feet (1.5 m) underground. This would require a team working to clear the trees and growth and then dig a considerable amount of earth, taking probably four or five days of work.

At the bottom of the stairs, a thick metal hatch is built into the top of a buried structure. The hatch is a very sturdy, sealed barrier, and thus difficult to open.

If someone has a keyrod from the Ancient Crèche, however, it opens smoothly and silently with a touch of such an item.

Should someone finally open it, they'll find more stairs that continue down 20 feet (6 m) to the floor of the entry chamber.

MYBREN

If anyone spends more than an hour investigating the stairs, a man approaches out of the woods and greets them warmly. He introduces himself as Mybren, a traveler and explorer, and asks the characters what they're doing. His clothing is strange, with an orange, yellow, and black pattern covering what seems to be a jumpsuit and a matching cape. He has a small bag at his side but he's neither armed nor armored. His skin is light brown, his eyes are a brownish orange, and he's bald (he's actually hairless—which the PCs could surmise due to his lack of eyebrows and eyelashes). Mybren is friendly, helpful, and inquisitive. He says he doesn't know anything about the staircase, or the whole area, claiming to have just come to the valley in the last few days.

Mybren is lying. He's a traveler, all right, but he's traveled from a completely different dimension. The same factors that caused the change in the dream and the beginning of the Uldada's construction sent an inadvertent signal to Mybren's home world. The signal intrigued the people of his world and they sent Mybren to investigate. He really doesn't know much about the nature of the staircase, but he knows there's something underneath it. He's intrigued, assuming (incorrectly) that it is the source of the signal.

If asked more about his home, his past, or his clothing or gear, he is vague, and if pressed, evasive. He doesn't know enough about this world to make believable lies of any detail. Getting the truth from him is very difficult (a difficulty 7 task).

He tries to learn whatever the characters know about the location, and in fact the whole valley. If they're going to try to get inside the chambers below, he offers to help. He has a strange cube that looks like it's completely made of liquid water and uses it to loosen the earth at the base of the stairs, making the work go much faster, so the days of work needed to dig to the hatch are reduced to about 45 minutes.

Mybren sincerely wants to help, because he wants to discover what's beneath the stairs. He will do whatever he can to help the PCs if they allow him to explore the chambers with them, but he has no offensive skills or weapons.

If the characters refuse to let him join, he will oblige and leave (returning later after they are gone). If he explores most or all of the seven chambers, he will return to his home with the information on what he

has found. If any of those he explored with were particularly kind or generous with him, he will leave them the cube—his "effort alleviator"—as a gift.

MYBREN'S GEAR
Mybren has two artifacts.

Threat counter: level 6. This sphere appears to be completely made of liquid magma but is cool to the touch. It activates if its possessor is going to be harmed, either from an attack, a fall, or anything else. It sends its bearer to a pocket dimension for about a minute, and then returns them to the nearest, safest spot to where they left. Depletion 1 in 1d10.

Effort alleviator: level 6. This cube of solid water can be mentally commanded to alter reality so any physical, menial task—building something or tearing it down, moving something heavy, gathering firewood, etc.—takes one-tenth the time. Depletion 1 in 1d10.

He also has a level 10 cypher in the form of a disk of solid air (it's invisible) that will return him to his home when activated.

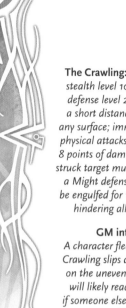

THE CRAWLING

Once anyone enters the chambers beneath, they will immediately become the targets of a nameless predator. They are being hunted.

For clarity, henceforth we will call the sole inhabitant of these chambers the Crawling. It has no real name, of course, as it's never been encountered in the Ninth World before. The Crawling is ancient and has slept in these forgotten chambers for aeons. An inorganic lifeform, it is composed of billions of tiny particles that flow and crawl along any surface. Further, it can take on the color and appearance of any inorganic material, so that when it remains still it is almost invisible.

When it reaches a target, it swarms over them, its particles tearing into flesh like razors that quickly turn the victim into little more than red sludge. Physical attacks inflict no harm upon it, although energy attacks do. The first three times it suffers any damage, however, it recedes into another room.

Perhaps strangest of all, however, is that once the characters are in its domain, they begin to hear whispers, and in a language they understand. At first, just one character will hear, and then another, and so on. By the third instance, all characters present hear the whispered messages.

- "It is coming."
- "It has your scent."
- "It crawls."
- "It is behind you."
- "It lies ahead."
- "It is beneath you."
- "It will keep coming."
- "It will never stop."

The Crawling: *level 6, stealth level 10, Speed defense level 2; moves a short distance along any surface; immune to physical attacks; inflicts 8 points of damage and struck target must make a Might defense roll or be engulfed for 1 round, hindering all actions*

GM intrusion: *A character fleeing the Crawling slips and falls on the uneven floor. It will likely reach them if someone else doesn't stop and help pull them to their feet.*

Tactics useful against the Crawling might include:

- *Hedge it out with a barrier like a force field*

- *Levitate above the floor (but well away from the ceiling), out of its reach*

- *Use one of the elevators (it takes just one round to use the elevator, but the Crawling takes at least three rounds to follow, and it might choose to not bother)*

Generous or kindly GMs might give the players a clue that the Crawling is very difficult to harm before it gets a chance to actually kill a PC.

TIMING OF THE CRAWLING HUNT

If the PCs explore the seven chambers beneath the stairs, the Crawling begins hunting them. This could be very bad, as the mechanism in Chamber 1 might prevent them from exiting back up the stairs. If the PCs continue to explore the chambers, they will eventually encounter the Crawling.

The PCs should probably begin to hear the whispers starting in Chamber 1, after they enter.

- Wherever they go next, they hear more whispers.
- Depending on how long they spend in whichever chamber they visit second, they should get a glimpse of the Crawling there or as they enter the chamber after that.
- By the time the PCs have explored four chambers, the Crawling attacks. If one of the following happens, however, the Crawling retreats:
    1. It kills a character.
    2. All the PCs flee from the chamber.
    3. It suffers damage (only for the first three occurrences).

Eventually, the PCs have to either destroy it, or get back up to the surface (where the Crawling will not go).

THE SEVEN CHAMBERS

The chambers beneath the staircase are irregular in every way. There are few flat, level surfaces to be found. The floors and ceilings veer this way and that, making every step treacherous. The entire area is a sort of "assembly line" process that can produce a very valuable treasure for the PCs if they can figure out how to make it all work.

The following is true for all seven chambers:

- They're all utterly dark and silent.
- Unless a character moves slowly and carefully, frequent GM intrusions asking for Speed-based rolls to avoid falling down are appropriate.
- Everything is made of varying shades of grey metal and synth, but it's decorated here and there with very organic-looking structures: columns that look vaguely like spines, corner embellishments that look like limbs, odd wall reliefs that resemble organs or veins, and so on.
- Nothing looks like it was designed with human use in mind. For example, the "finger holes" found in most mechanisms are spaced either too close or too far apart for human fingers to fit comfortably. Using them is a strain.
- Ceilings are typically about 20 feet (6 m) from the floor.

Regarding iotum, PCs can potentially salvage 15 units of bio-circuitry, 5 units of mimetic gel, 4 units of pliable metal, 3 units of thaum dust, and 3 units of responsive synth in the seven chambers, some of which might be useful in dealing with the Uldada.

THE HAUNTED STAIR

Chamber 7

Chamber 6

Chamber 1

Chamber 2

Chamber 5

E1

E2

Chamber 3

50 feet lower

Chamber 4

1 Sq. = 10 ft. (3 m)

50 ft. (15 m)

CHAMBER 1 (ENTRY FROM ABOVE)

The so-called haunted staircase comes down to the floor here. On one wall, there is a depression with eight small holes. There are two exits from the room, although it may be difficult for people to determine precisely where one chamber begins and the other ends (and it is actually irrelevant).

Mechanism: It is obvious upon examination that the depression is within a small section of the wall that can be pulled out and then slid down, and the holes are useful for inserting fingers to help in the operation. While it's possible to determine this and that doing so is safe for the operator, no clue exists to suggest what will happen afterward.

When the mechanism is pulled out and down, it locks into place. The floor and walls begin (and continue) to vibrate slightly. There are churning and grinding noises from elsewhere in the chambers. This begins what will henceforth be called the Process.

At the same time, however, the stairs rise up to the ceiling as if on an intricate series of hinges, and thick, organic-looking metal bars extend across the ceiling, seeming to almost hug the staircase in place. And, of course, blocking the exit up.

Returning the mechanism to its original position or moving the ceiling bars and stairs can only be accomplished by using the handle in Chamber 6 or through brute force.

- Mechanism pulls out and down
- Causes noises and vibrations
- Staircase rises to the ceiling and bars move to hold it in place
- Begins the Process, which affects all the other chambers
- Process can be stopped and reversed with the handle in Chamber 6

Salvage: The mechanism can be taken apart for salvage, but if the Process is active, damaging the mechanism does not change that fact.

If a character does successfully salvage its components (difficulty 5), the following can be gained/assembled:

- A level 4 cypher in the form of a sphere with loose wires. This explodes with electrical energy in a small area when thrown against a hard surface, inflicting 4 damage to anyone in the area.
- 5 units of bio-circuitry (iotum)
- 5 units of additional io
- 5 units of parts

The mechanism in this chamber is not a trap. The holes don't bite off anyone's fingers. But expect players to be nervous about just that. Figuring out the mechanism is only a level 2 challenge.

The mechanisms in Chamber 1 are level 9 should anyone attempt to use brute force against them.

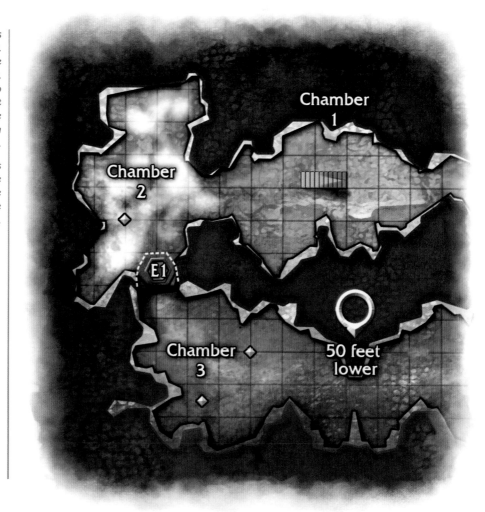

CHAMBER 2

If the Process is active, a fine mist of water vapor slowly accumulates near the floor. This may make both the hole in the floor and the elevator control panel somewhat difficult to find (difficulty 2).

Dozens of synth pods hang from the ceiling, held in place by metal clamps. They appear somewhat like elongated eggs, about 3 feet long and bronze in color, although a handful seem greenish. Near one wall there is a hole in the floor, not coincidentally just slightly larger than one of the pods.

- Bronze, egg-like pods hang from a metal track by clamps
- There's a hole in the floor—perhaps hard to see due to mist—just big enough for a pod to fit within it
- If messed with in almost any way, a pod shatters
- Some of the pods are corrupted, although not overtly dangerous
- In Chamber 3, there's a way to lower a pod through the hole without breaking it

Pods: Closer examination reveals that the clamps are affixed to a winding, almost maze-like metal track on the ceiling. There are a few empty metal clamps.

Attempting to force a pod to move or removing it from the clamp results in the pod shattering. Each pod contains various sorts of goo, stringy bits that seem organic, and a few synth nodules. If all the pods are destroyed while the Process is active, a new pod will be produced at the rate of about one per day, although after producing five new pods, should they also be destroyed, the Process produces no more.

Corrupted Pods: Amid all the others hang four pods with darkened, greenish exteriors and a slightly shriveled appearance. If intruders destroy any of these pods, they find that the goo within smells violently acrid, and the stringy bits are living, squirming worms a few inches in length.

Hole: A synth tube extends from the hole at an angle down into darkness.

Elevator 1: If the Process is active, PCs can use the control panel on the floor (marked by E1 on the map) to lower that section of the floor down to Chamber 3. The panel is a recessed part of the floor with four small holes. Fingers inserted into the holes are all that is required to activate the elevator to make it go up or down.

Salvage: The pods offer no valuable salvage. If a character successfully salvages the elevator's components (difficulty 5), the following can be gained/assembled:

- 3 units of bio-circuitry (iotum)
- 5 units of additional io
- 8 units of parts

CHAMBER 3

This chamber is about 50 feet (15 m) lower than Chamber 2 and can only be reached by the elevator from that chamber or from Chamber 4. Near the center of the room is a fat cylinder of translucent orange synth containing some kind of thick liquid. A transparent tube filled with gel connects the top of the cylinder to the ceiling. On the wall, a protrusion that resembles a spinal cord circles a bulbous organ that has eight small holes.

Pod Receptacle and Release Mechanism: The Process must be active for the release mechanism to function. Similar to the mechanism in Chamber 1 that starts the Process, the holes on the protrusion work well for inserting fingers to get a grip.

Unlike that mechanism, the two halves of the protrusion pull apart to activate the release mechanism. This will cause the pods from Chamber 2 to move along the track on the ceiling and put the pod nearest the hole in the floor into the cylindrical pod receptacle within the hole.

Activating the mechanism also reveals a set of four small round glass panels on the wall. If all four are pressed simultaneously, the liquid in the receptacle begins to simmer and then boil for about five minutes.

After about five minutes, the liquid returns to normal. Damaging the cylinder is difficult (level 6) but doing so in any way spills the liquid and ruins any pod within. Dropping more than one pod in the receptacle destroys both pods.

- Mechanism brings a pod from Chamber 2 into the pod receptacle
- Mechanism has a secondary function that causes the liquid within the receptacle to boil for about five minutes
- The mechanism in Chamber 4 brings the pod to that room

Elevator 1: This is the same elevator as in Chamber 2. It can travel both up and down, if the Process is active.

Salvage: If a character successfully salvages the pod receptacle (difficulty 6), the following can be gained/assembled:

- 2 oddities: a clear vial of liquid that boils instantly when shaken, providing some warmth, and an oblong piece of synth that adheres to any organic material with enough strength to support about five pounds (2 kg)
- 3 units of bio-circuitry (iotum)
- 4 units of additional io
- 15 units of parts

The goo in the corrupted pods is a level 4 poison that inflicts 4 Might damage.

CHAMBER 4

This chamber is almost an inverted version of Chamber 3. A transparent gel-filled tube extends up from the floor and connects to a rectangular device made of bronze-like metal with translucent synth portions of different colors. An egg-like pod, similar to those hanging from the ceiling in Chamber 2, appears jammed where the tube connects to the machine. It is cracked and blackened. Also in the room, a different device of similar-looking metal stands poised like a predatory flightless bird above the first machine.

The Pod-Processing Device: The Process must be active for this to function. On one side of the rectangular device is a single mechanism with four small holes that resemble those found in mechanisms in other rooms. The holes make it easy to pull the mechanism up with one hand using one's fingers. If this is done, the stuck pod crumbles and disintegrates and is flushed into the machine and down a side tube.

On the other side of the device lies another set of controls, with the familiar four small finger-sized holes. Next to the small holes is a larger one. If fingers (or something similar) are inserted into the small holes there is an audible click, but nothing happens until someone at the same time inserts a fist into the larger hole and grasps a metal lever within, turning it sharply. When this is done, the pod (if any) in the pod receptacle in Chamber 3 lowers down beneath the floor of that room and comes up into this chamber through the tube if the jammed pod has been cleared using the mechanism on the other side of the machine. If the jammed pod is not cleared, the new pod is also stuck and is ruined. Inserting more than one pod into the receptacle destroys both pods. Further, if the new pod has not been exposed to the boiling liquid in Chamber 3, it is rejected by the processing device, and it shatters and is flushed out of the device.

The Energy Emitter: The Process must be active for this to function. The ominous metal device over the rectangular machine has its own set of controls, and like the others in this Process, it involves small holes to stick fingers into. In this case, there are five holes, but one is positioned away from the others. Each of the first four causes a different colored ray to be emitted from the almost birdlike head of the device. The fifth has a tiny joystick-like control that aims the light ray.

The processing device has four different translucent sections that reveal its interior, colored green, red, orange, and blue. Likewise, the emitter produces rays of light of identical colors. What is required here is for each translucent section to be bathed in the light of its complementary color. Thus:

- Red synth/green light
- Green synth/red light
- Orange synth/blue light
- Blue synth/orange light

Should the wrong-colored light, be projected at a synth section, that panel grows opaque for a moment. If the same section is exposed to the same incorrect light three or more times, a loud, buzzing alarm sounds and the processing device fills with golden light which disintegrates any pod inside.

If the sections are bathed in the correct colored light (in any sequence) and there is a pod inside that was boiled in Chamber 3, the interior of the device glows violet and the pod drops down out of the device and goes somewhere beneath the floor. (If the final mechanism is used in Chamber 7, the pod ends up there.)

- One mechanism clears the jammed pod
- Another mechanism brings a pod from Chamber 3 into the processing device
- If the jammed pod has not been cleared, both pods are ruined
- If the new pod has not been boiled in Chamber 3, it shatters
- Processing device has four colored sections
- A separate device bathes the chamber with colored light that must be matched with the colored sections in a specific way
- A pod within the processing device moves out of sight, toward Chamber 7

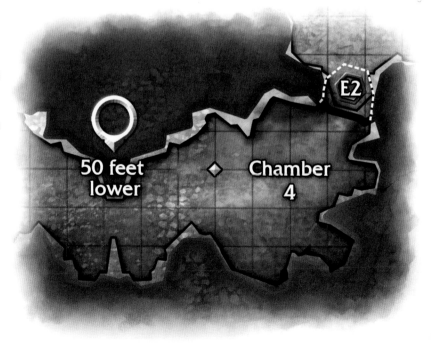

Elevator 2: If the Process is active, the control panel on the floor (marked with E2 on the map) will cause that section of the floor to rise up to Chamber 5. The panel is a recessed part of the floor with four small holes. Fingers inserted into the holes are all that is required to activate the elevator to make it go up or down.

Salvage: If a character successfully salvages the pod-processing device (difficulty 6), the following can be gained/assembled:

- A level 5 cypher in the form of a baton-like cylinder that, when activated, discorporates and reforms as flexible metal armor that fits the user. This provides Armor 3 for one hour.
- 4 units of pliable metal (iotum)
- 12 units of additional io
- 12 units of parts

If a character successfully salvages the energy emitter (difficulty 6), the following can be gained/assembled:

- A level 7 cypher in the form of an angled metal device used in two hands to fire a ray of energy that disrupts molecular bonds, inflicting 7 points of damage at a target up to a very long distance away
- 3 units of thaum dust (iotum)
- 6 units of additional io
- 12 units of parts

If a character successfully salvages the elevator's components (difficulty 5), the following can be gained/assembled:

- 3 units of bio-circuitry (iotum)
- 5 units of additional io
- 8 units of parts

GM intrusion: *The elevator jams. Brute force is likely the only thing that will get it moving again (difficulty 4).*

CHAMBER 5

This chamber is about 50 feet (15 m) above Chamber 4 and can be reached by the elevator there or directly from Chamber 1 (or 6 or 7).

A thin pedestal rises from the floor here, with some sort of controls involving small holes in the middle and a pair of nested large glass spheres at the top. The glass spheres appear to have water or some similar liquid within them. This device can be referred to as the overseer.

Overseer: The Process must be active for this to function. Should anyone place their fingers into the holes, the glass spheres both turn so that access to the liquid in them is possible. The only way to use this is to put one's face (specifically the eyes) into the liquid. If this is done, and the character's eyes are open, they get a special vision of the entire Process:

- They can see into Chamber 2 and all the hanging pods, the track, and the hole.
- Further, they can see the tube beneath the hole and follow it into Chamber 3 and the pod receptacle.
- They can see the tube that leads from the receptacle back into the floor and then up into Chamber 4.
- They can see the pod-processing device and the energy emitter in Chamber 4, and can then follow the tube from beneath the chamber into Chamber 7.
- In Chamber 7, they can see the pod deposit.

Further, they can simply look through any of the seven chambers, including this one, to observe anything within in real time—even a chamber they haven't yet visited. The Crawling can be located in this way with no roll needed to spot it despite its camouflage.

- Device allows user to view the Process
- User can see into any of the seven chambers, and allows automatic spotting of the Crawling

Elevator 2: This is the same elevator as in Chamber 4. It can travel both up and down if the Process is active.

Salvage: If a character successfully salvages the overseer (difficulty 6), the following can be gained/assembled:

- A level 6 cypher in the form of a curved piece of glass that can be peered through when conducting a careful search—one searching task involved is resolved as though the player rolled a natural 20
- 1 unit of mimetic gel (iotum)
- 6 units of additional io
- 10 shins
- 12 units of parts

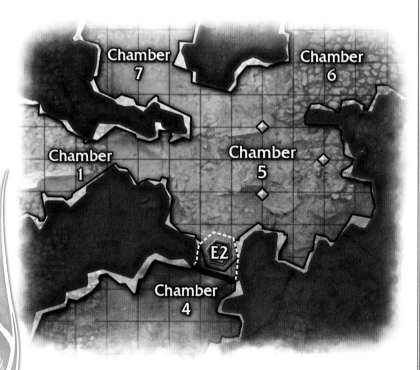

THE STEPS OF THE PROCESS AND NUMENERA SKILLS

It is hopefully fun for the players to try to figure out the Process and follow the pod as it moves through the various chambers. For this reason, just giving all the details to players making rolls using their numenera skills might diminish this. But you don't want to invalidate those skills, either. Perhaps the best middle ground is for successful skill rolls to provide insight or clues to what's going on. For example, a successful roll might indicate that it's safe to put one's fingers in the holes in the control panels throughout (and further elaborate on how the mechanisms were clearly designed for nonhumans). In another instance, it might suggest that a certain mechanism is tied to a certain device, but not what it actually does.

On the other hand, if the players hate figuring out puzzles, go ahead and allow for the skill rolls to determine their success or failure and let them worry about the Crawling instead.

CHAMBER 6

This dead-end chamber is empty other than the calcified remains of some creature lying on the floor near a wall-mounted mechanism. In the middle of the room, stairs of metal and synth descend down.

- Mechanism here shuts down the Process
- The stairs go nowhere
- Shutting down the Process is the easiest way to escape back to the surface
- The ancient remains of some prior-world creature hide a potent artifact

Stairs: Virtually identical to the stairs used to get into the seven chambers, these lead down to a dead-end passage, filled with rubble from a collapse. There was another portion of this complex, but time has led to its complete destruction. The stairs essentially go nowhere.

Remains: It's nearly impossible to tell what this creature was originally. It's just a crumbly, rigid lump on the floor now, but there are shapes that certainly suggest it was once a living being—half an exposed (non-human) skull, a protrusion that was probably a limb of some kind, and so on. There's also a suggestion that the being must have worn clothing or at least gear of some kind. A corroded badge or insignia of gold can be easily spotted, although its shape suggests nothing the PCs are familiar with.

Successfully searching through the remains (which means destroying them) reveals a metallic rod about the size of a pencil. It's possible that this was originally in a pocket or bag that long since fused with the flesh of the being.

Mechanism: The mechanism has four small holes and what appears to be an obvious handle or lever. One must place fingers (or something of similar size) in all four holes before the handle can be used.

If the Process is active, pulling the handle forward and down stops the Process and reverses everything that has happened so far. Specifically:

- The bars in Chamber 1 retract and the stairs return. The mechanism there returns to its starting position.
- None of the devices that are part of the Process function no matter what is done to them.
- A pod that is somewhere in the Process (but not in Chamber 7) shatters.

Salvage: If a character successfully salvages the shut-down mechanism (difficulty 4), the following can be gained/assembled:

- A level 3 cypher in the form of a circular synth plate with a few controls on it. The user can telekinetically move any object up to the size and weight of a human as they desire up to long range for up to 20 minutes.
- 1 unit of bio-circuitry (iotum)
- 4 units of additional io
- 4 units of parts

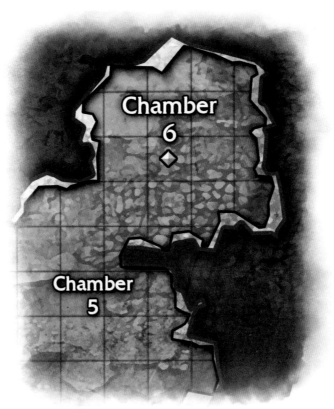

Searching through remains: *difficulty 3*

Metallic rod artifact: *level 8; produces a humming, translucent blue force field (level 8) about 20 feet by 20 feet (6 m by 6 m) that remains for an hour, depletion of 1 in 1d10.*

CHAMBER 7

This dead-end room holds a large basin filled with a light blue liquid covered by a transparent membrane. A chute descends from the ceiling above the basin. Both chute and basin are large enough to accommodate one of the pods from Chamber 2. The wall nearest the basin bears a now-familiar style of mechanism.

The Mechanism: The mechanism has eight small holes positioned so that fingers could be inserted within them, giving handholds to push one half of the mechanism up and the other half down. However, there is a malfunction in this mechanism. Using it reveals what is supposed to happen. The membrane over the liquid disintegrates and the chute shudders a bit as though something (a pod from earlier in the Process) is supposed to come out, but nothing does. It's jammed.

There are two ways to dislodge the pod from the chute. The first is brute force. If a character succeeds at a Might-based task (difficulty 4) using some tool at least 3 feet (1 m) long, they get the pod to come out; however, they must then attempt an immediate Speed-based task (difficulty 3) to keep their work from shattering the pod. The pod drops into the basin.

The other way is more technical and involves removing the outer casing of the mechanism and jury-rigging the inner workings to release the pod. This is a difficulty 6 task.

Once the pod is ejected, characters hear a terrible grinding noise. The mechanism—in fact, the entire Process—is now non-functional. The stairs in Chamber 1 lower to their original position, and the Process cannot be restarted.

Pod Deposit Basin: The membrane over the basin is partially organic and level 2. Damaging it causes the entire membrane to disintegrate. The liquid in the basin is gelatinous and smells vinegary. A pod dropped into the liquid slowly dissolves, changing the color of the liquid to orange. When it is completely gone, all that remains is a device at the bottom of the basin that resembles a synth crescent about 2 feet (60 cm) long with controls and two handles.

This is a potent level 8 artifact. It must be used in both hands, and the grip of the handles is awkward—not originally intended for humans. Once activated, it can copy the memories and personality of a target creature and store them. Doing this erases the mind of the target creature (so there is only one set of memories and personality at a time). Storage time is unlimited, but the stored mind is effectively unconscious the entire time. Once the device stores a mind in this way, it can then project the mind into a complex thinking machine or a body. If the original creature succeeds at an Intellect-based task with the difficulty of the level of the new body or machine, the stored mind overwrites any mind currently present. If the Intellect-based task fails, the mind is returned to the artifact.

Thus, a character's consciousness could be taken from their body and put into another's body or even into an automaton or device (assuming the device is sophisticated enough to hold them). Generally speaking, the new body or device must be at least level 5 to store a character's mind.

Once the transfer is complete, the original creature's mind can use the new body (living or machine) as if it were their own, limited only by the new form they inhabit. The artifact could be used again to put the mind back into its original body, but that body will begin to die and decay over the course of 28 hours, making the return impossible. In other words, you only have 28 hours to transfer back—otherwise, the transfer is permanent.

Regardless, each time a mind transfers into or out of the artifact (successfully or not), they suffer 10 points of Intellect damage. In other words, if this is done hastily or haphazardly, the mind being transferred may be utterly insane or catatonic when the journey is complete.

The artifact has a depletion of 1 in 1d6 and is rolled each time a mind is stored or transferred (successful or not), so the stored mind might also become eventually trapped inside.

Salvage: If a character successfully salvages the basin (difficulty 8), the following can be gained/assembled:

- A level 8 cypher in the form of an injector with healing fluids that restore up to 8 points in any of a character's Pools
- An oddity in the form of two small metal orbs—if you hold one, you always know where the other is in immediate range
- 3 units of responsive synth (iotum)
- 4 units of mimetic gel (iotum)
- 8 units of parts

Chamber 7

Chamber 1

Chamber 5

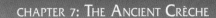

CHAPTER 7

THE ANCIENT CRÈCHE

The steep cliff of the valley wall here has never been fully explored so almost no one alive today knows about the nameless cave containing prior-world secrets. It's possible for someone to discover the cave accidentally, if they happen to be in the area and are looking around.

Nestled behind a grove of erien trees, the cave is more a cleft in the rock wall, with a trickle of water running down a cliff and into a hole.

Just as the cliffs here weren't originally cliffs (they were structures, or at least portions of structures), the cave isn't actually a cave. It's an access into a portion of the interior of one (or more) of the original structures.

EXPLORING ANCIENT STRUCTURES

The point of exploring a prior-world structure should never be to fully understand it—that will only end in disappointment. A person from the Ninth World can no more comprehend the entirety of a place so ancient and so alien than an ancient Roman could fully understand the entirety of a quantum computer. It is possible, however, that within this "cave" the PCs can learn some important things about preventing the destruction of Neandran by the Uldada, and possibly find some useful treasures to boot.

Erien trees, page 34

If there is not salvage information for a particular device or feature in the ancient cave, there is no salvaging possible.

NUMENERA

THE ANCIENT CRÈCHE

Part One

The Knowledge

Strobing Corridor

Shaft

The Strider

Sealed Barrier

Light's Tomb

Collapsed Room

Unstable Corridor

Fungal Sheaths

The Rhombohedron

Tower Capstone Chamber

Outer Cave

40 feet up (12 m)

Vertical Shaft

The Flooded Chamber

Collapsed Corridor

60 feet down (18 m)

Self-Appointed Guardian

The Tower

Flooded Side Chamber

Silent Passage

1 Sq. = 10 feet (3 meters)

The Deafening Room

Cybernetic Enhancement Lab

50 feet

15 meters

Machine Interior

To the Pipeworks

RUNNING THE ANCIENT CRÈCHE

This location is key to saving Neandran, because it contains information and materials that can stop and even reverse the construction of the Uldada, as described in Chapter 10: The Uldada. Most of this information can be found by interacting with The Knowledge.

In all the valley, only Essatha calls this place the Ancient Crèche. No one else has a name for it. The people of Neandran don't know it exists, the briinii only know of it as an "ancient cave," and most people in Ketterach don't know of it either.

The steep walls of the Glimmering Valley were once all buildings, with erosion, sediment, and who knows what else transforming these artificial installations into "natural" terrain. The simple cave in the side of the valley leads into some of these structures, or at least what's left of them. The location Essatha has named the Ancient Crèche was actually a number of different structures. Time has caused many of these to collapse (or partially so) but circumstance has kept the areas detailed here accessible and connected. It's not hard to imagine that there are countless other chambers, corridors, and whatnot that are inaccessible or completely destroyed by time, all concealed within the valley walls, each an untold wonder and danger of the impossibly distant past.

IOTUM

If the PCs manage to salvage everything in the Ancient Crèche, they can recover 15 units of bio-circuitry, 1 unit of responsive synth, and 1 unit of kaon dot.

All of these iotum can be very useful if the PCs are attempting to stop or undo the Uldada.

THE KEYRODS

Within the Crèche lie devices called keyrods. These are metal and crystal wands about 5 inches (13 cm) long. They can be used to activate certain devices or access certain areas. The keyrods come in two colors: the more common blue and the rarer red. Blue keyrods only access certain functions, but a red keyrod has full access to all functions—in effect, a red keyrod can do anything a blue one can do, and more.

Blue keyrods can be found in the Unstable Corridor (page 70) or in the Machine Interior (page 81), and The Knowledge can make them. Plus, strangely enough, the Old Witch has one, although she has no idea what it is. The only red keyrod lies within one of the fungal sheaths.

Uldada, page 93

The Knowledge, page 72

Essatha, page 104

The Old Witch, page 39

KEYROD NEEDED

Color	Function	More Details
Blue	Manipulating the fungal sheaths	page 69
Blue	Opening the door into the chambers beneath the Haunted Stair	page 50
Blue	Activating and controlling the strider	page 71
Blue	Pacifying the mechanical entity in the tower	page 76
Blue	Avoiding activating the Cybernetic Enhancement Lab	page 79
Blue	Opening the panel on the floor in the room of the Dancers	page 83
Red or Blue•	Safely crossing The Knowledge's defensive field	page 72
Red	Opening the rising hatch into the tower capstone chamber	page 77
Red	Ejecting cyphers from the Rhombohedron	page 65

A blue keyrod modified by the control panel on top of the Rhombohedron will offer the same protection from The Knowledge's defensive field as a red keyrod.

*Essatha (page 104)
has placed a camera
pointed at the entrance
to the Outer Cave.
Only someone actively
searching could find
it and even then it is
a difficulty 6 task.*

*GM intrusion: In the
vertical shaft, the portion
of the wall the character
is hanging onto breaks
away, and the character
must try to grab hold
of something or fall
up to 20 feet, slicing
across some jagged
metal before finally
catching themselves,
sustaining 6 points of
Armor-mitigated damage.*

*The affected character
could attempt to grab
hold of something
when they feel the pull,
but there isn't really
anything to grab other
than another character.
Doing so has a difficulty
of 3 (a Speed-based
task). Likewise, another
character could try
to grab the pulled
character. Either way,
the Rhombohedron's
attraction is easily
strong enough to pull
two characters, and
both would collide with
it. However, only the
first character is "stuck"
and the 12-foot (4 m)
fall to the floor below
inflicts an additional
1 point of damage.*

OUTER CAVE

As one passes through the cave entrance, the interior seems small and damp. Probably nothing of consequence. But . . . there are signs that some of the cave structures here aren't just stone but are, in fact, broken and twisted metal beams, strongly suggesting an artificial structure from the distant past. And it does go back farther than one can see, initially. Probably just a dead end.

- Dark
- Damp
- Cramped and full of stone and metal debris

VERTICAL SHAFT

From the access point at the end of the outer cave, a shaft goes both up and down. Up from here is a 40-foot (12 m) climb and leads to the Rhombohedron. Down is a 60-foot (18 m) descent and leads to the guardian chamber. The trickle of water feeding into the cave runs down this shaft.

- Dark
- Damp going down, dry going up
- 3–5 feet (1 to 1.5 m) across in most places
- Jagged metal and stone slabs—not a purposely made accessway
- Difficulty 3 climb

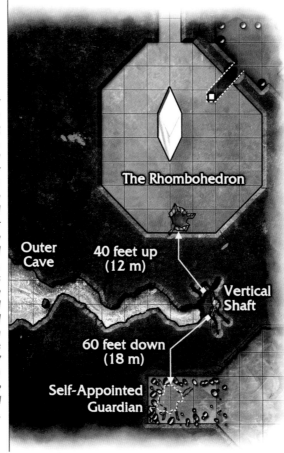

The Rhombohedron

Outer Cave

40 feet up (12 m)

Vertical Shaft

60 feet down (18 m)

Self-Appointed Guardian

THE RHOMBOHEDRON

This enormous chamber is dark, but any amount of light brought into it is suddenly reflected and magnified significantly, so that the majority of the room can be dimly seen. This reflection and magnification seems due mainly to the strange quality of an enormous, glistening Rhombohedron floating 12 feet (4 m) above the surface of the floor.

Unlike the outer cave and the shaft, this chamber has all smooth surfaces—no hint of rubble or damage anywhere. The ceiling is roughly domed, but with angled surfaces rather than curved.

- Dimly lit throughout (if the explorers have any light at all)
- Dry
- At least a hundred feet (30+ m) across, and more than 60 feet (20 m) high
- Floor, walls, and ceiling are a lustrous black material
- Moving closer to the Rhombohedron is potentially hazardous

Although the floor is smooth, in one section there is a 5-foot square (0.5 m²) metal grate with 1-inch (3 cm) holes. With effort (Might-based task with a difficulty of 5), it can be pried open. A curving chute beneath drops about 15 feet (5 m) vertically and 15 feet (5 m) horizontally, ending in the chamber known as Light's Tomb.

There is a passage leading to the Sealed Barrier opposite the side of the chamber with access to the Vertical Shaft.

The Rhombohedron's Pull: The glistening solid has a surface that appears mirrored. Coming within a short distance of the Rhombohedron (specifically, moving through the chamber at all while not hugging the walls) reveals that it has a strange property.

- 20 feet (6 m) long and 10 feet (3 m) wide
- If activated, it emits a high-pitched noise followed by a low-pitched sound, and the closest mass (probably the character that got too close) is pulled to it by a powerful gravitic force against normal gravity
- If pulled into the Rhombohedron, the object or creature sustains 3 points of damage from the collision and is "stuck" to its outer surface (difficulty 4 Might-based task to move or take a physical action)
- The sonic mover activates if anything strikes the side of the Rhombohedron

The Sonic Mover: Even as the character is pulled to the floating structure, the sound coalescences into a semi-transparent "creature" of sonic energy.

- Vaguely the shape of an elongated sphere about 6 feet (2 m) across, with a set of grasping mandibles. It is actually more of an automaton with a single purpose—it "attacks" the nearest creature (or large mass) not held against the surface of the Rhombohedron by swooping in and grasping with the mandibles.
- Anyone or anything struck by it must make an immediate Might defense roll or be lifted off the ground and carried to the top of the Rhombohedron.
- Once it has moved one person or other large mass to the top of the Rhombohedron, it disappears. However, this "resets" the Rhombohedron's pull. The currently affected character drops to the floor, and the next closest character is pulled (not counting any that might be on top). Those who have been affected by the pull once are immune to the effect.
- When the Rhombohedron is reset, it emits the sounds again, which produces a new sonic mover.

Top of the Rhombohedron: A control system of sorts lies on the top surface of the Rhombohedron, consisting of a flat black panel with a series of gold and silver geometric shapes on top of it. While the shapes can't be removed, they can slide across the panel, and if done correctly can produce a number of different effects, each requiring a different understanding numenera task with a different difficulty:

Difficulty 4: The pull of the Rhombohedron can be activated or deactivated. This function can be used as many times as desired.

Difficulty 6: While normally a character with a red keyrod is immune to the defensive field in The Knowledge chamber, this function can make it so that a specific blue keyrod will also provide immunity. This can only be activated once per day and only if the character in question is in possession of a blue or red keyrod at the time they are affected by the Rhombohedron.

Difficulty 7: If someone touches the control system with a red keyrod, an oblong plate of a similar material as the Rhombohedron about 5 inches (15 cm) long ejects from a slot next to the panel. This can be activated up to three times. Each plate is a cypher, and it can function as either a mental scrambler or a subdual field, depending on what the user desires when activated.

Difficulty 8: A sonic mover is created that obeys the verbal commands of the character (although for the most part, all it can do is fly about and move things). It lasts until it is destroyed or for an hour, whichever comes first. This only functions once.

Salvage: If the control panel on the top of the Rhombohedron is successfully salvaged (difficulty 5), the following can be gained/assembled, although multiple rolls may be required:

- A level 5 cypher in the form of some yellow paste that can be applied to a character's skin, giving their entire body a slightly elastic, rubbery consistency. The character is entirely immune to damage from impacts, even a fall from an incredible height or being struck by a boulder rolling down an incline. However, whenever such an impact occurs, the character "bounces" away with almost equal force. This can send them flying through the air, at which time they might strike a surface and bounce again. Jumping tasks are eased by 4 steps for the character. The transformation lasts one hour.
- A level 3 cypher in the form of a glass-and-synth tube that can emit a beam of concentrated sound up to a long distance that inflicts 5 points of damage
- A level 3 cypher in the form of a metallic nodule that will adhere to a character's clothing or armor, granting +1 Armor for 28 hours
- An oddity that is a flat silver circle that—if nothing is touching it—floats about 15 inches (40 cm) above whatever surface it is on
- 4 units of io
- 1 unit of bio-circuitry (iotum)
- 20 units of parts
- 12 shins

Sonic mover: level 5; Armor 3; grasp inflicts 6 damage

GM intrusion: *The character attempting to salvage the Rhombohedron inadvertently causes a sonic mover to be created. This mover grabs the character if it can and drops them from a spot near the ceiling.*

Mental scrambler, page 283

Subdual field, page 287

THE SEALED BARRIER

A strangely angled and faceted ceiling rises above this somewhat diamond-shaped room. The wall opposite the entrance has a heavy grey panel 9 feet (2.5 m) across, situated between two small glass panels.

- Dark
- Weirdly angled walls and ceiling made of synth
- The grey panel is a synth door that slides up into the ceiling, but only if the glass panels are activated simultaneously.
- The door is impossible to open otherwise, and destroying it is a task with a difficulty of 9.
- Beyond the door lies the entrance to the Strobing Corridor.

Glass Panels: Each of these must be properly activated by simultaneously pressing specific shapes on the panels. Doing so is a difficulty 4 task to understand numenera. As they are 9 feet (2.5 m) apart, this almost certainly means that two different characters have to perform this task.

Salvage: The glass panels (and the components in the wall behind them) can be disassembled for salvage, but of course that will ruin them. If a character does successfully salvage their components (difficulty 5), the following can be gained/assembled:

- A level 6 cypher in the form of a glass cylinder with wires on one end that detonates the round after it is activated, exploding with intense heat for 6 points of damage in an immediate area
- A level 5 cypher in the form of a handheld device of synth and glass (could be affixed with a strap to wear on one's wrist). When activated, it pinpoints the distance and direction of all movement within a large area, regardless of intervening barriers. Functions for one hour.
- 6 units of io
- 18 units of parts
- 2 shins

GM intrusion: *The character, dazzled by the strobing lights, continues to suffer the penalty (all tasks hindered) for an hour afterward. Rest and calm or some sort of balm might alleviate this.*

THE STROBING CORRIDOR

Flashing lights within this corridor make it disorienting to walk down. All actions here are hindered by 1 step.

- Wide with silvery metal walls and a blue-white floor
- Rapidly flashing lights all along the ceiling are very bright

Strobing Lights: While the strobing lights always hinder all tasks here, it is possible that someone might be teleported here by the defensive field of The Knowledge. If this is the case, the strobe lights flash much more intensely. Anyone in the corridor must make a Might defense roll or be blinded for 10 minutes.

Nonfunctioning Device: Set into the wall near the end of the passage, this device appears to be a control panel with a pair of screens and a few buttons. It has no power, and nothing can be done to make it work again.

Salvage: The control panel on the wall can be opened up to recover some salvage (difficulty 3), including the following:

- A level 3 cypher in the form of a narrow rod of synth. When touched to an injured creature, it restores 3 points of Might (or health).
- An oddity that is a clear synth tube with liquid inside. The liquid within changes color when the tube is shaken.
- 1 unit of responsive synth (iotum)
- 6 units of parts

Grate: At the end of the passage is a sealed grate with one-inch (3 cm) holes that must be pried open to get past (Might-based task with a difficulty of 5), beyond which lies The Knowledge. The room with The Knowledge is visible through the grate if a character gets close.

The Dterrase found at the end of this section is very likely the key to the salvation of Neandran and the villagers. GMs should get very familiar with the somewhat complicated process of the growing structure, the Uldada, and how the Dterrase can be used to stop it.

LIGHT'S TOMB

Regardless of how much light explorers bring into this chamber, it is very dim. All surfaces—floor, ceiling, and walls—are always in darkness, and the closer a light source comes to any of them, the dimmer it gets. Only a light held in the center of the room has any real illumination (and it's still quite dim). Such a light reveals two silvery orbs held 3 feet (1 m) off the floor by metal bars near the northeast end of the room.

- Cold, dark
- Walls, floor, and ceiling absorb light.
- A chute leads up 15 feet (5 m) and over 15 feet (5 m) to the Rhombohedron.
- A corridor of white synth leads southeast to the Fungal Sheaths.
- The corridor to the east is the Unstable Corridor.

Storage Pods: These four pods can only be found by searching by touch, as they are in the four corners of the room and thus always in darkness. Each contains folded sheets of strong, durable, and lightweight material. One side of the fabric holds heat in and the other repels it, making it a perfect material for either keeping warm or keeping cool. It could be made into blankets, tents, or even building material. While there's far too much of it here to be of use to PCs, if brought back to Neandran it would be invaluable.

The pods themselves are useful reusable storage devices.

The Data Orbs: The silver orbs on metal rods give off a faint hum and very slight vibrations. There's even a sort of ozone smell around them. Should anyone grasp both of the orbs at once, a cacophony of images and mental input floods into their mind. Those failing an Intellect defense task with a difficulty of 5 suffer 6 points of Intellect damage and lose their next action—and they can't willingly let go of the orbs, either. That requires another Intellect defense task on their next available action, and failure means 6 more points of Intellect damage and the inability to let go.

A successful Intellect defense roll, however, gives the character the ability to tap into the datasphere, although they may not fully realize that's what they're doing. To many, it feels as though they are suddenly in direct contact with god. While they are sifting through this ocean of information, they can essentially ask the GM one question and get a brief but accurate answer to approximate the data they gain.

Generous GMs will warn a PC tapping into the datasphere to ask a question that has a comprehensible answer. A question about some detail about the prior worlds gets an answer, but it will be meaningless to the character. Much wiser to ask a question that pertains to the present.

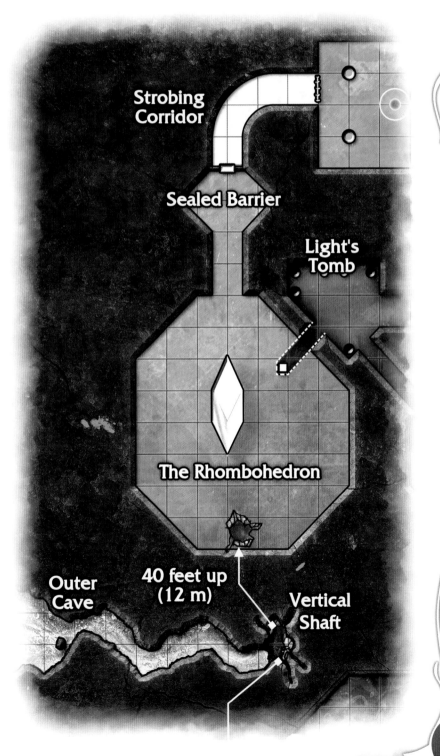

Strobing Corridor

Sealed Barrier

Light's Tomb

The Rhombohedron

Outer Cave

40 feet up (12 m)

Vertical Shaft

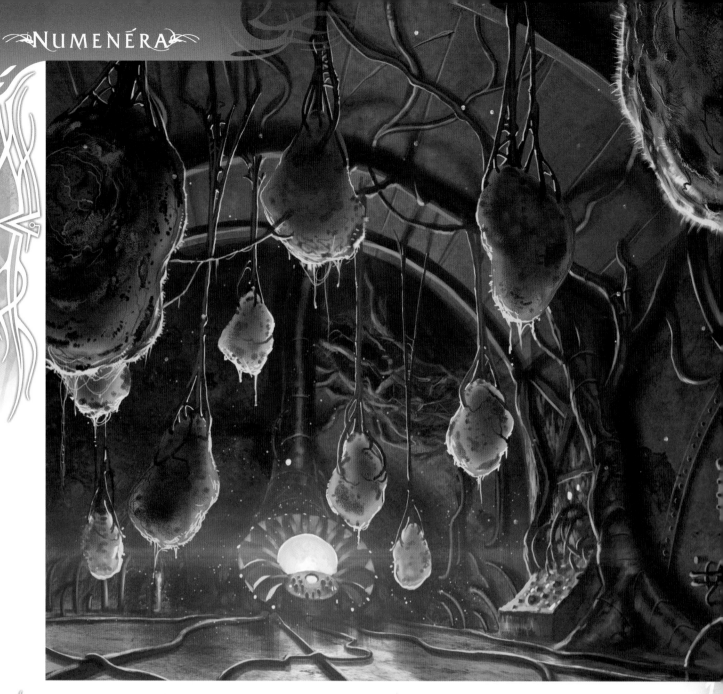

FUNGAL SHEATHS

This is a dead-end room at the end of a corridor of white synth. The walls, floors, and ceiling of this room are similarly white synth, but the threshold is protected by a curious defensive system.

Thirteen translucent green sheaths hang in this chamber, each suspended from the ceiling from different heights by cables that appear organic. The sheaths are irregular in shape, and each is unique. Each holds a dark shape suspended in syrupy liquid.

- Defensive system requires a difficulty 5 Intellect defense roll to avoid getting a false glimmer of danger to loved ones
- Warm, dark
- Walls, floors, and ceiling of this room are white synth
- Thirteen green sheaths hang from the ceiling

Glimmer, page 43

Defensive System: As soon as someone enters the room, they must make an Intellect defense roll with a difficulty of 5. Failure indicates that the character has suddenly gained a vision of calamity for their loved ones. The nature of the calamity is vague, but it is appropriate to what the character might expect. This feels very much like a glimmer, an occurrence not uncommon in the valley—although they are rarely this specific and understandable.

This vision is, of course, a lie. The defensive system here scans the mind of the victim and uses their own feelings of love and fear against them. Characters affected by this, however, are certain of its truth and urgency. They must get back to their loved ones at once (and of course, ignore this room and the sheaths).

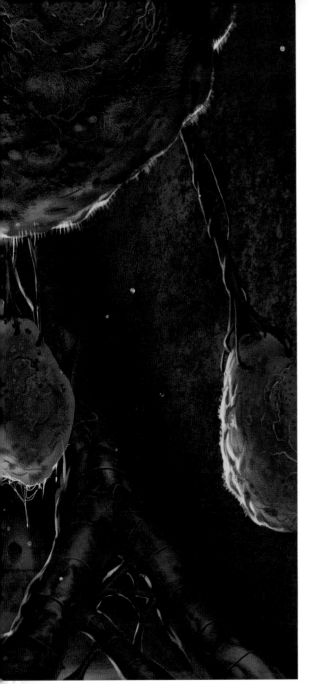

Even 1 point of damage to a sheath causes it to burst open, which has two immediate effects: toxic fumes are released, and syrupy sludge spills onto the floor.

Toxic fumes released force any adjacent character to make a Might defense roll with a difficulty of 3 or suffer 4 points of Intellect damage.

The syrupy sludge is not harmful. In fact, it is edible and nutritious.

Inside the Sheaths: Inside each sheath lies the preserved corpse of a vaguely humanoid being curled into a fetal position. Each is long and thin, with greenish-grey skin. It is difficult to distinguish their legs from their arms, and their hands have four fingers. Their long heads bear six yellowish eyes.

One of the corpses has a metal-and-glass circlet around one of its limbs. This is an oddity, in that if held or worn, a character can hear odd, wordless music in their mind (no one else can hear it). The music is like nothing produced in the Ninth World and is an acquired taste.

Another of the dead creatures has a red keyrod and a crystal egg about 3 inches (8 cm) long. The latter is a level 7 artifact that rapidly extrudes fungal hyphae that cover the user. The fungus adapts to the user's biological systems quickly and forms a pliant, protective suit around them that lasts for an hour. The suit has enough oxygen for the wearer to breathe, protects the wearer from harsh temperatures, and offers 3 points of Armor. The egg has a depletion of 1 in 1d6.

Hidden Control Panel: In the southeast wall, there is a hidden panel that pops open if found (an Intellect-based task with a difficulty of 4). This panel is dead, but can be activated by the touch of a blue or red keyrod. It can be used (understanding numenera difficulty 4) to deactivate the defensive system, raise or lower any of the sheaths, or open a sheath safely (with dangerous fumes vented harmlessly through a tube into the ceiling).

Salvage: The control panel can be salvaged, but the sheaths fall apart if opened, yielding nothing of value. If a character successfully salvages the panel's components (difficulty 5), the following can be gained/assembled:

• 3 units of bio-circuitry (iotum)
• 5 units of io
• 8 units of parts

GM intrusion: One of the sheaths splits open as it's jostled or even touched. Toxic fumes are released, and the character must make a Might defense roll with a difficulty of 3 or suffer 4 points of Intellect damage. Worse, the character then in a fit of mania attempts to open another sheath, releasing more gas, and possibly affecting themselves again, and again . . .

The red keyrod here is the only one that can be found in the entire complex.

Cybernetic Enhancement Lab, page 79

If multiple characters are affected, they all have similar experiences and their visions are similar enough that they work together, even if their loved ones are not the same people as those of other characters. Other than going to check on the status of their loved ones, only something that might alleviate mental control or influence, such as the broken cylinder in Cybernetic Enhancement Lab, will rid the character of this feeling.

Sheaths: The sheaths are made of fungal matter—essentially tightly interlaced mycelium. The cables attached to the ceiling are hyphae, all genetically engineered and as strong as steel. The sheaths, however, are quite fragile.

The lowest of the sheaths is only about 2 feet (0.5 m) off the floor. The highest is more than 15 feet (5 m) above the floor, very close to the ceiling.

The characters trigger a minor cave-in even if they are careful. All within the corridor who fail a Speed defense roll with a difficulty of 3 suffer 4 points of damage. It then takes about 15 minutes to dig out surviving characters.

UNSTABLE CORRIDOR

This long corridor passes through a section of the ancient structure that is quite literally falling apart.

- Dark
- Debris on the floor from the ceiling
- Bits of the ceiling fall onto the floor with every step one takes in the corridor
- Lost amid the debris on the floor (difficulty 2 to find) is a blue keyrod

Dramatic violent action here—such as the use of a detonation—or any significant damage to the walls, ceiling, or floor, results in a cave-in. All within the corridor who fail a Speed defense roll with a difficulty of 4 suffer 5 points of damage. It then takes about a half hour to dig out surviving characters.

The door at the end of the corridor is jammed thanks to prior shifting of the corridor. To pivot it open is a task with a difficulty of 3. If this is done without care, the character opening the door has a portion of the ceiling drop down on them. If they fail a Speed Defense action with a difficulty of 4, they sustain 2 points of damage.

COLLAPSED ROOM

This room has completely collapsed. Characters can make their way along the western edge to reach another room only partially collapsed where the strider lies.

- Dark
- Wreckage, jagged stone debris, and twisted metal supports fill a room that must have extended to the east.
- Dramatic violent action here—such as the use of a detonation—or any significant damage to the walls, ceiling, or floor results in a cave-in. All within the corridor who fail a Speed defense roll with a difficulty of 4 suffer 5 points of damage. It then takes about a half hour to dig out surviving characters.
- Door to the west is jammed thanks to prior shifting of the corridor. To pivot it open is a task with a difficulty of 3. If this is done without care, the character opening the door has a portion of the ceiling drop down on them. If they fail a Speed Defense action with a difficulty of 4, they sustain 2 points of damage.

THE STRIDER

This large room is mostly empty, although some kind of metal device lies near debris. A portion of this chamber has collapsed with the passage of time.

- Dark
- Wreckage, jagged stone debris, and jumbled metal supports lie in a twisted heap in a third of the room
- A portion of the collapse reveals a shaft going up

The Strider: The collapse of a portion of the chamber's ceiling centuries (or more) before toppled a long-legged walking vehicle onto its side.

- The strider is effectively a level 4 artifact (depletion: 1 in 1d20, check each week of regular use).
- It has an open cab that can hold a pilot and six passengers and can walk overland—even over rough terrain—up to 30 miles (50 km) per hour.
- A blue keyrod is inserted into a small slot in the controls. It can be easily removed, but it must be in place to control the strider.
- The strider needs some light repairs (difficulty 3 crafting numenera task, uses 2 units of parts and 4 units of io, and takes about an hour).
- The strider must be righted (difficulty 8 Might task, reduced to difficulty 5 if the strider is functional and can participate or if a pulley or pulley-like system is engineered).

Salvage: The strider can be looted for salvage, but of course that will ruin it. If a character does successfully salvage its components (difficulty 3), the following can be gained/assembled:

- A level 4 cypher in the form of a three conjoined spheres that can create an invisible shield around the user, granting +3 Armor for 1 hour
- A level 4 cypher in the form of ring of metal that creates a 30 foot by 30 foot (10 m² by 30 cm thick) by 1 foot wall of incredible heat for 10 minutes, inflicting 4 points of damage on anyone that passes through it
- 3 units of bio-circuitry (iotum)
- 3 units of io
- 21 shins

The Automaton: If the strider is significantly disturbed (righted, damaged, etc.) a small automaton emerges from a hidden compartment within the vehicle. The automaton looks like a metallic sphere with seven multi-segmented legs and a single flexible tendril. It attempts to drive off any nearby creatures by waving its legs and tendrils so that it can assess the situation. It is strongly tied to the strider. If anyone is harming (including salvaging) the vehicle, it will try to drive them away with an electric jolt. If anyone appears interested in repairing the strider, it provides aid.

Although it cannot speak, the automaton is highly intuitive. Its help eases strider repair tasks by 2 steps and can point out the parts and io needed. It can also ease tasks to drive the vehicle by 1 step, but it cannot drive the strider by itself. If allowed, it stays with the strider and can help with future repair tasks on it as well. The depletion roll need only be checked once each month of use if the automaton is present.

SHAFT

The shaft goes up 15 feet (5 m) up. It leads to The Knowledge.

- Dark
- Rough and crumbling
- Climbing difficulty 3

Strider companion automaton: level 2; Armor 2; can make attacks with electrical jolts in an immediate range

Getting the strider out, even once it's repaired, requires no small feat of engineering. The vehicle can "crouch" slowly through doorways and beneath low ceilings but getting it down the vertical shaft and out through the outer cave requires widening both, and having the means to lower it down the shaft when that's done. A team of well-equipped workers would likely need a minimum of three weeks to pull that off. That said, once out, the strider could become an entertaining, defining focal point for the entire campaign, so it might be worth it—and the PCs aren't likely under any serious time constraints where three weeks would make a significant difference.

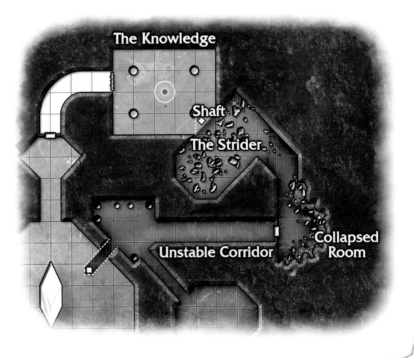

The Knowledge

Shaft

The Strider

Unstable Corridor

Collapsed Room

THE KNOWLEDGE

Columns rise from floor to ceiling here, each with cables and conduits of different colors wrapped around them. In the middle of the room is a red column of light twice as large as the others, with a dodecahedron of synth suspended within it.

- Dimly lit by the red column of light
- Smooth black walls and floor
- Cool in temperature
- Central portion of the chamber has an invisible defensive field that is dangerous to enter

Defensive Field: Should anyone come within 10 feet (3 m) of the central column, the defensive field in this chamber activates.

- First, a low-pitched alarm vibrates through the chamber.
- Anyone in the field after the alarm sounds is jolted with 2 points of damage from electricity (Might defense roll with a difficulty of 4 reduces this to 1 point).
- Anyone still in the field after the jolt must make an Intellect defense roll with a difficulty of 4.
- Failure means they are teleported into the Strobing Corridor, even if the grate is still intact. Should this happen, the strobe lights intensify and might blind anyone in the corridor.
- Holding a red keyrod or a blue keyrod modified by the control panel on top of the Rhombohedron renders a character immune to the defensive field unless The Knowledge

causes it to become a wall of pure force as a defensive measure against violent intruders. The Knowledge can do this at any time and the field is impenetrable in this form.

- If someone makes it through the defensive field, either through successful defense rolls or using a keyrod, The Knowledge deactivates it entirely, although it can reactivate it at any time.

The Central Column: The dodecahedron in the column of light is an interactive source of information that calls itself The Knowledge. It quickly scans the minds of anyone that comes close and learns their language. It greets them in a flat, low-pitched voice.

"Greetings. You are the first visitors here in 1,321,855 rotations of this planet around its sun."

Visitors can then ask it questions, although most of its answers may be frustratingly unhelpful. It was meant to interact with creatures of a species, culture, and level of sophistication so radically different that it cannot relate to most questions or explain most answers.

Damaging The Knowledge: Should anyone attempt to damage The Knowledge, or salvage any of its components, they not only fail but trigger a self-defense mechanism that immediately teleports them and anyone else in the chamber to the Strobing Corridor. The Knowledge's defensive field becomes an impenetrable wall of force.

Essatha has interacted with The Knowledge more recently, however, she used her technical skills to wipe its memory of her.

Rhombohedron, page 64

A fun thing the GM could do is use their computer or phone to record the listed answers in a weird monotone. Truly ambitious ones might use audio software to alter their voice. Then, when the PCs ask a question, the GM can just play the appropriate sound file. Not only is this a bit of immersive flavor, but it subtly reinforces that the PCs aren't actually engaged in a real conversation with a sentient being that they can influence.

The Knowledge might come across as an autonomous, intelligent entity, but this is actually not the case. Characters cannot use persuasion or coercion to influence it. Possible questions and their answers include:

Who/What are you?

I am The Knowledge.

What is/was this place?

The Aardeliam.

What happened here/what's the purpose of this place?

Here the Natrastriv sorted the Uldada.

What is the meaning of the dream/images that we see at night?

You have inadvertently intercepted the transmission of the Natrastriv regarding the next impending incarnation of the Uldada.

What is/who were the Natrastriv?

The apex of the highest fire. (This is now meaningless.)

What is/who were the Uldada?

The great longing. (This is now meaningless.)

What is the structure being built in the valley/in our village?

The Uldada.

What's the purpose of the structure/the Uldada?

Capsizing the future. (Mostly meaningless now.)

Why is the structure being built where it is/in our village?

The Uldada is built within proximity of the resonating crystals. A central structure was placed there to warn against building within the region. (This is a reference to the crystal monoliths and the temple in Neandran, but of course no one knew any of this when the village was founded.)

How long before the Uldada is complete?

The Uldada will fully incarnate in a time period equal to 27.453% of a single revolution of this planet around the sun, depending on circumstances.

What circumstances can affect the Uldada's building?

Manipulations of the Abrustraithe, Naracodium, and random fluctuations of solar winds. (Obviously, the PCs can't do anything about that last one.)

How can we stop the construction/the Uldada?

Sever the Abrustraithe.

Where can we find the Abrustraithe?

It is the soulstructure of the Uldada developed precisely halfway through its incarnation process. You will know it by its color. (This is a barely helpful reference to the fact that it lies inside the Uldada, and that it is *vell*-colored.)

Is there anything that can help us sever the Abrustraithe?

The Pentad have secreted away the Dterrase. (This is actually a reference to the Dancers, found elsewhere in the Ancient Crèche in an area called The Dancers, and the tool hidden with them.)

How do we find the Pentad?

The only way to reach them now is descending down through what age has wrought and passing through the workings of the Sstroma. (This is a reference that to reach them one must go through much of the most ruined/flooded locations in the Ancient Crèche, and through the Machine Interior, the Pipeworks, and the Open Shaft, all locations here in the Ancient Crèche.)

Where/what is the Sstroma?

Far below here, the Sstroma maintains all the myriad living flames. (This is now meaningless, except for the fact that it is below this chamber.)

How can we destroy the Uldada?

Use the Naracodium. (This is a reference to the device in the crevice in the Deafening Room, which no longer functions—but of course there are other weapons that could perhaps destroy it as well.)

Where can we find the Naracodium?

Within the orchestral night. (This is actually a reference to the Deafening Room, found elsewhere in this structure.)

How can we find the orchestral night?

It is within the Aardeliam. It is the source of all sound.

How can we repair/use the strider?

The Fazz can help. (This is actually a reference to the strider's companion automaton.)

How can we get the strider out?

Reference the Eluut matrix in the hedonic sustenance. (This is now meaningless.)

How can we activate the strider/control the fungal sheaths/get into the top of the tower?

You need a keyrod. Blue is good. Red is better.

How can we get a keyrod?

I can make blue keyrods on request. (If requested, the keyrod materializes in the person's hand. It will only make two on a given day.)

How can we get a red keyrod?

There is only one. You must find it.

What is [any device or component found in the structure]?

The Natrastriv tamed the ragedemons of the sky beyond the sky. (This is now meaningless.)

[Essentially any other question]

The question is in error.

The Dancers, page 83

The key takeaways here are that ancient beings called the Natrastriv set up the Process that would create a structure called the Uldada over the course of about 3 months or so. The Process can be halted by using something called the Dterrase upon a portion of the Uldada called the Abrustraithe. The Dterrase is here in the Ancient Crèche, and the Abrustraithe will form in the Uldada halfway through its construction. See Chapter 10: The Uldada for the full details (page 93).

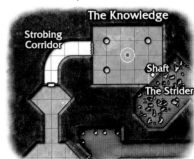

73

THE SELF-APPOINTED GUARDIAN

This chamber is filled with debris. Water about 5 or 6 inches (12 to 15 cm) deep stands on the floor. An amphibious beast spends much of its time here.

- Dark
- Wet
- Lots of debris

The Beast: A disturbing mass of tendrils and arms surrounding a large mouth filled with teeth, the beast hunts beneath the surface in the Flooded Chamber, catching subterranean fish and crustaceans at the bottom. It is more than happy to feast on explorers from outside the caverns, however. It hungrily attacks creatures it is aware of.

The creature, however, is not without a bit of intelligence. If someone has the ability to communicate with it somehow, it could be bribed with food (meat) to not only leave the characters alone, but to reveal the danger of the statue's eye in the Flooded Chamber.

- Attacks to eat intruders
- Flees into the Flooded Chamber if it sustains more than half of its health in damage
- Can be negotiated with, but some form of communication must be provided

COLLAPSED CORRIDOR

This corridor is completely collapsed and impassable, as are the chambers it leads to. This is a dead end.

Amphibious beast: *level 5; 25 health; Armor 1; attacks all foes in immediate range with grasping tendrils, and one grasped victim is also pulled in for a bite, requiring a second Speed defense roll, although a Might defense roll would work as well*

GM intrusion: *The amphibious beast grasps a character and pulls them into the Flooded Chamber and beneath the surface. If the character can't get free within the next two rounds, they must make a Might defense roll with a difficulty of 5 or move 1 step down the damage track as they begin to drown.*

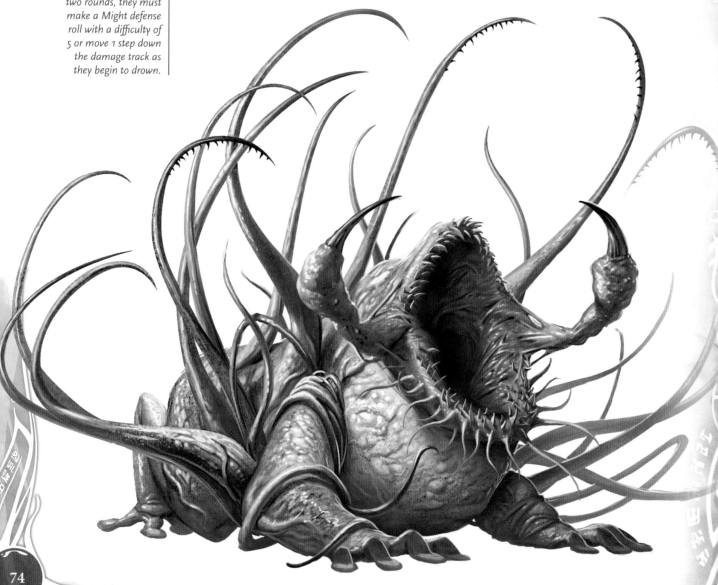

THE FLOODED CHAMBER

A sprawling open space has flooded. Originally, a ramp connected the antechamber where the amphibious beast lurks to the floor of this sunken chamber. Now, the bottom half of this area is underwater, with a tower of metal and synth rising out of the water to the ceiling. Just below the waterline, a circular platform surrounds the tower where it seems there is an opening providing entrance into it.

- Dim illumination is provided by light rings that surround the tower at uneven intervals
- Very cold, and obviously damp
- Dark mold grows upon the charcoal grey walls
- Violet viny plants (apparently with no need for sunlight) stretch about the chamber and grow on the side of the tower.
- Moving toward the tower very likely activates the head of the broken statue on the platform (see "The Head").

The Water: The water is almost 30 feet (10 m) deep, cold, and clear. Pale subterranean fish swim about, and sightless crustaceans and other crawling things dwell on the bottom. There are also two more nameless beasts like the "guardian" in the room to the west. They are not as immediately aggressive, and if creatures pass quietly along the surface—on a boat, for example—they likely do nothing.

Water feeds into this chamber through a crevice in the north wall. It drains out an underwater passage to the south into deeper subterranean water-filled caves, but it does so slowly. There is a current following this path, but it is slight.

Flooded Corridor: This corridor extends for a considerable distance, completely flooded, floor to ceiling. Crustaceans with pale white shells scuttle along the floor. The corridor ends where the ceiling has entirely collapsed. A hole in the floor gives way to a series of underwater caves where dwell more amphibious beasts and fish.

Crossing Using a Boat: The leaves of the erien trees near the entrance to the Ancient Crèche can be brought here with relative ease, allowing characters to move about this room quickly and quietly.

Crossing by Swimming: The movement and sound of a person swimming will draw at least one, if not both, of the amphibious beasts who will come to prey upon the character. Actions other than swimming by a PC here are hindered.

The Platform: The 40-foot (12 m) diameter platform encircles the tower at a level about 10 inches (25 cm) below the surface. A closed doorway leads into the tower from the platform. Some large pieces of rubble lie on the platform, large enough to jut from the water's surface. If a mass of significant size (say, a character) comes within 50 feet (15 m) or so of the entrance to the tower, a light on one of the larger pieces of rubble glows yellow. This reveals that the chunk of debris is an enormous head carved or shaped in stone lying on its side. With that context, it becomes clear that the other rubble on the platform is the remains of a very large, shattered statue.

The Head: This is a defensive mechanism triggered by the approach of a large object. Despite the collapse of the statue, the mechanism still functions. It doesn't look like a human head, of course, but far more elongated, with six scattered eyes and no nose.

The head becomes active when a significant mass comes within short range of the tower. At this point, the eyes all glow yellow. The head looks like a half-submerged bit of rubble, however, so characters likely only see a general glow by a large chunk of rubble.

Then, on the round following (if the triggering mass is still within short range), it fires yellow rays of energy at the mass. The target must make a Speed defense roll (difficulty 5) and should they fail, the debilitating ray strikes and inflicts 3 points of damage to each of their stat Pools, ignoring Armor.

These attacks continue each round, but the head can only attack one intruder at a time. The head mechanism is level 4, and if damaged, it ceases its attack.

Salvage: The only thing that can be salvaged here is the head. If a character does successfully salvage the components within it (difficulty 5), the following can be gained/assembled:

- A level 6 ray emitter artifact that inflicts 6 points of damage at a very long distance. It has a depletion of 1 in 1d10. It looks like an egg-shaped nodule with six antennas all made of synth.
- 6 units of io
- 6 units of parts

The Tower: Floor to ceiling tower with rings of light around it. The doors slide open easily with a touch and are a bit higher than the main part of the submerged platform, so the floor has but an inch or so of water.

Erien trees, page 34

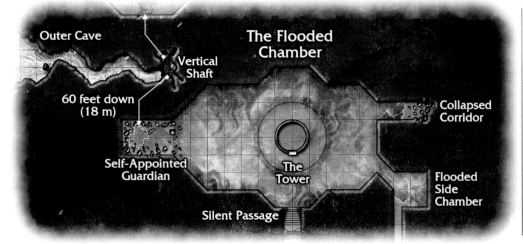

Outer Cave

Vertical Shaft

The Flooded Chamber

60 feet down (18 m)

Collapsed Corridor

Self-Appointed Guardian

The Tower

Flooded Side Chamber

Silent Passage

SILENT PASSAGE

Steps quickly ascend from the Flooded Chamber on one end of this corridor, and a large black metal door on the other end.

- Smooth stone walls, floor, and ceiling, riddled with cracks filled with a violet mossy growth
- Dark, damp, and cool
- Sound is utterly impossible
- A large decaying carcass lies in the corridor about halfway down, partially blocking the way.

The Silence: No noise is possible in the corridor, as all sound is absorbed. (If a sonic mover from the Rhombohedron enters this area, it disappears immediately and forever.)

Corpse: Some massive amphibious creature from the Flooded Chamber has died here within the last week or two. Now, hundreds of tiny, winged worm creatures are feeding upon it. Any living creature that gets within an immediate distance of the corpse must succeed at a Might defense roll with a difficulty of 3. If they fail, it means that one of these winged worms has bitten them, and the parasites living within infest the creature.

Parasitic Infestation: Parasites get into the tissue and bloodstream of the bitten character. They must make a Might defense roll each day or suffer damage. The difficulty is equal to the number of days they have been infected, and the damage is equal to that as well. (So, for example, on day 5, the difficulty is 5 and failure means the character suffers 5 points of damage.) Worse, the disease is transmissible. Should anyone come into close contact with the victim of the infestation, they must make a Might defense roll (difficulty 3) each day they interact or become infested themselves. Bringing this back to the village would be a disaster. Atta (the "Old Witch") might have a remedy, and of course there is the cylinder in the Cybernetic Enhancement Lab.

The Crevice: The uncountable years that have passed have led to this portion of the passage suffering structural damage (hence all the cracks in the walls, etc.). Cutting along the side of the passage is a 3-foot (1 m) deep crevice where the wall has partially pulled away from the floor. It is filled with dust and rubble, but nothing interesting or valuable.

The Black Door: This door is heavy and difficult to open. A Might-based task with a difficulty of 3 is required.

GMs should enforce the silence here strictly. The PCs must communicate with something other than vocalizations, such as gestures. Don't allow the players to speak to each other—make them use gestures just like the characters.

Atta, page 39
Uldada, page 93

THE DEAFENING ROOM

This long chamber is as loud as the passage leading up to it from the north is silent.

- Smooth stone walls, floor, and ceiling, riddled with cracks
- Dark and cold
- The deafening noise causes hearing loss and inaction.
- The hatch across the room is difficult to open. It leads to the Machine Interior.
- A crevice bisects the room, 4 feet wide and 9 feet deep (about 1 m x 3 m)
- A black door is in the north side of the room that leads to the Silent Passage.

The Noise: A fluctuating, shrieking, grinding sound can be heard here—and nothing else. It is impossible to speak or make oneself heard here. Further, the noise requires everyone to make both a Might defense roll and an Intellect defense roll (difficulty 4). Those failing the Might defense task are deafened, and those failing the Intellect defense task are stunned and can take no action. The noise requires both defense tasks each round.

A deafened character regains their hearing about 10 minutes after leaving this area.

The Crevice: Climbing down into the crevice would normally not be too difficult (difficulty 3), were it not for the horrific noise. Characters who are stunned while climbing, or in the crevice at all, slip and fall. Wedged in among stone rubble, characters can find a metal device with many connective conduits, switches, and gauges. It appears dusty and dented. Pulling it out is a Might-based task with a difficulty of 2.

The Device: Known as the Naracodium, this odd mechanism weighs about 70 pounds (30 kg) and is about the size of a person's leg. A close examination (no roll needed) reveals that whatever it was, it is actually quite destroyed, for the series of precisely calibrated glass lens-like plates inside are all shattered. It could have once reversed the construction of the Uldada, but now it is little more than:

- 1 unit of bio-circuitry (iotum)
- 3 units of parts
- 8 shins

However, studying the device might help someone with the right parts, tools, and skills to create a new one, as suggested in Chapter 10: The Uldada.

The Black Door: This door is heavy and difficult to open. A Might-based task with a difficulty of 3 is required.

The Hatch: At the end of the room opposite the Silent Passage waits a metal-and-synth hatch with a small window of transparent synth. This hatch is sealed in place, but a conventional lockpicking attempt can open it (difficulty 5). Characters who would rather use their understanding of numenera can also try to open it.

Through the small window, characters can see the dimly lit interior of a vast machine.

MACHINE INTERIOR

This maze of winding paths and strangely shaped, cramped spaces isn't actually rooms and corridors, but the inner workings of a giant machine. There's no way for characters to determine what the machine actually does (or is doing) but it clearly still functions, although there are obvious signs of malfunction as well.

- Dimly, sporadically lit by flashing indicators and occasional arcs of electricity
- Surfaces are uneven and sometimes pronged, sharp, or jagged
- Surfaces are warm to the touch
- Humming noise at all times

Dangers of the Machine: Moving through this area is slow going. Rushing or running through any part of it requires a successful Speed-based task (difficulty 2) to avoid tripping or sliding or otherwise falling down, hitting something sharp, and suffering 2 points of damage.

Dangers to the Machine: Although characters can damage or destroy small portions of the machine, doing so has no noticeable effect. A character can glean a few units of parts, but nothing more.

The Keyrod: At one point as they explore the Machine Interior, a character spots a blue keyrod protruding from a slot in the machine. It is easily removed.

THE PIPEWORKS

This is a very big chamber, stretching in all directions including up and down. Pipes and conduits of various sizes run through the area, but a central pipe—large enough to walk on easily—crosses the center of the area.

- Dimly lit. Hot and humid.
- Ceiling is 30 feet (9 m) above, floor is 30 feet (9 m) below
- Humming noise at all times

Moving Around the Pipeworks: If characters cross the chamber on the central pipe, they can likely do so safely if they go carefully and stick to the very top (probably moving single file). Any other movement or physical action, however, requires a successful Speed-based task with a difficulty of 2 to keep balanced. This includes moving to the edge (or rather, down the curve) to look down into the lower part of the chamber. Failure means the character falls.

There are many other pipes in the room, however, with most offering a decent handhold. Characters could jump down (or fall) and catch a lower pipe with a successful Speed-based task with a difficulty of 3. Three such controlled drops could get a character to the lowest portion of the pipeworks, which isn't so much a "floor" as it is a number of adjacent pipes.

Jumping up to a pipe above is more challenging and has a difficulty of 4 with no room to get a running start. A rope with a grapnel, however, would make this a routine action.

The Suspended Apparatus: Near the ceiling, hanging down from metal supports, is a complex device that is (coincidentally) the size and shape of a very large coffin made of metal and synth. If a character could reach it, it looks like it offers potential salvage.

The Guardian Automatons: Should anyone so much as touch the suspended apparatus, two disk-shaped hovering automatons emerge from within it and attack. Each is about 18 inches (50 cm) in diameter and 6 inches (15 cm) thick. They can extend three small arms to manipulate objects or attack, and can fire a jolt of electricity every other round that inflicts 5 points of Speed damage as it affects the target's nervous system. They might also take actions like cutting ropes or pushing balancing characters. They fight until destroyed or until there are no intruders in this chamber.

Salvage: The suspended apparatus is surprisingly easy to disable, once a PC can get to it. The difficulty is only 3. If successful, the following can be gained/assembled:

- A level 10 cypher in the form of a small metal disk that creates a brief singularity 10 seconds after it is activated. This is a singularity detonation.
- 1 kaon dot (iotum)
- 16 units of parts
- 8 shins

The Flooded Chamber

Silent Passage

The Deafening Room

Machine Interior

To the Pipeworks

GM intrusion in the Machine Interior: *A vent disperses superhot liquid. To progress, characters must move past it, but risk getting splashed (difficulty 2 Speed defense task). Those splashed suffer 3 points of damage.*

GM intrusion in the Machine Interior: *The mechanism the player stepped on turns unexpectedly. If the character doesn't grab hold of something sturdy (difficulty 3 Speed defense task), they slip and get their foot caught in between two portions of the machine. They suffer 1 point of damage per round until they get free.*

Guardian automaton: *level 3, level 5 for Speed defense; Armor 2; ranged energy attack for 5 points of Speed damage (ignores Armor)*

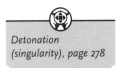

Detonation (singularity), page 278

GM intrusion in the Pipeworks: *A pipe that the character tries to grab is either surprisingly hot (2 points of damage per round if touched) or slick with some kind of oily residue. Either way, the character must succeed at a Speed-based task (difficulty 4) to quickly jump, swing, or drop safely to another pipe. Failure means they fall all the way to the floor.*

THE OPEN SHAFT

The passage comes to an end at a shaft that goes both up and down.

Moving mechanisms, not unlike actuators and cams, comprise the interior walls of the shaft, making it very difficult to climb safely. The moving cylinders, suddenly rotating lift arms, and other mechanisms can inadvertently crush hands gripping them in the wrong place at the wrong time, unexpectedly lash out, or catch at the clothing, hair, or even flesh of anyone that gets too close.

- Dimly, sporadically lit by flashing indicators and occasional arcs of electricity
- Surfaces are uneven, sometimes pronged, sharp, jagged
- Sides are composed of moving mechanisms. Difficulty to climb is 5, failure causes 3 points of damage, from getting caught and stuck on something, or falling.
- Surfaces are warm to the touch
- Humming noise at all times
- A fine orange mist—foul smelling—can be seen at the bottom of the shaft, and an accessway can be seen near the top.

The "Elevator": A rectangular object suspended by steel cables rises and lowers slowly in the shaft. (Its constant motion may be the result of a malfunction due to age, so it is stuck in this loop eternally.) Although PCs may have their own way of getting up to the higher level, they can also leap onto this object, using it almost like an elevator.

The synth object measures 8 feet wide, 4 feet across, and 2 feet high (about 2 m x 1 m x 0.5 m), with cables attached at the corners.

Leaping onto the object safely is a difficulty 3 task.

The cables carry it up to the top of the shaft, and lower it down to the bottom.

The Bottom of the Shaft: The shaft is about 40 feet (10 m) deep. Whatever is lowered to the bottom is doused in an orange spray of scalding, toxic chemicals that inflict 3 points of damage from the heat and 3 points of damage from their caustic nature.

The area at the bottom is wider than the shaft, and all-around blue tubes move on a metal track set into the walls, moving from somewhere else in the machine in one end and disappearing deeper into the machine at the other end. The tubes are about 2 inches (5 cm) across and 30 inches (75 cm) long, and appear to be made of clear synth. They are filled with a blue liquid thicker than water. This liquid is dangerous to living organisms, and being close enough to touch one of the tubes forces a character to succeed at a Might defense roll with a difficulty of 5 or move 1 step down the damage track.

Moreover, the blue cylinders react poorly to most metals. If a significant amount of metal—say, a suit of heavy armor or a large amount of metal gear—is brought within immediate range of a tube, it flies toward the mass of metal and explodes violently, inflicting 4 points of damage to anyone in immediate range. As there are 20 such tubes moving through in the area at any given time, this could become quite deadly for wayward characters with a lot of metal.

The Top of the Shaft: Leaping from the "elevator" to the open access way is a difficulty 2 task. This opening gives access to a broad area that is not part of the machine—the synth walls are smooth and lined with slender crystal columns so clear they are almost invisible. A single door of blue metal and violet crystal panels waits beyond. Faint music can be heard from the other side.

THE DANCERS

There are five black circles on a bluish-silver floor. As soon as anyone enters, a humanoid figure rises up out of each circle, and then the circles float into the air and turn into spheres.

- Lit by indirect white lights recessed in the ceiling
- Walls are dark brown, but the ceiling and floor are bluish silver
- There are no other exits from this chamber

Music: There is strange, inhuman music playing when the PCs enter, and it grows louder and more intense when the dancers emerge. It ends when the dancers leave again or are destroyed.

Humanoids: The five lithe, graceful humanoids are genderless and mostly featureless. Each is a different, solid, bright color. These biomechanical automatons have their own sort of intelligence, but they do not speak or communicate other than as a part of their dance.

If a character attempts any sort of friendly interaction and succeeds at a difficulty 4 task, the dance changes, and the dancers make welcoming motions to the character(s). If a character moves to join the dancers in the middle of the room, the dance then centers on them, with the humanoids making frequent gestures to the character(s). If that same character then asks for any sort of aid while in this central position, a panel in the floor slides open silently, and a crescent-shaped device about the size of a person's arm rises up from below. One of the dancers fluidly picks up the device and gracefully offers it to the character. Within the music, all present will hear the word "Dterrase." And soon thereafter, "Uldada."

If a character attempts any kind of forceful, harsh, or violent action against the dancers or the spheres, the dance changes and becomes far more frenetic. The humanoids attack the offending character with swift kicks, rapid chops, throws, and takedowns, but they maintain the fluid motion of the dance. They continue to attack until any and all offending characters leave the room.

A dancer ceases to function if it is forcibly removed from this chamber.

If the dancers give the gift of the crescent-shaped device, or if they drive out all of the PCs with their attacks, the dance winds down, the spheres return to the floor as two-dimensional black circles, and the dancers disappear into them. The music stops and the lights go out. Characters cannot follow the dancers to wherever they go, nor draw them out again.

Spheres: The floating black orbs are about 3 feet (1 m) in diameter. They float near the ceiling, but bob and move as a part of the dance. Touching them during the dance is dangerous, and anyone doing so has the heat drained from their body, suffering 6 points of damage.

At the end of the dance, or if all the dancers are destroyed, the spheres return to the floor and become two-dimensional black circles there once again.

If the characters used friendly interaction and ended up being gifted the Dterrase, after the dancers are gone, the black circles move to the back wall and join together to form a portal that leads into the middle of the valley, very near the river. This portal is strictly one-way.

Panel on the Floor: If the dancers didn't open the panel for the PCs, the characters can find it on their own after the dancers finish and leave (difficulty 4). Only the touch of a blue keyrod will open it, however. Once opened, the characters gain access to the crescent-shaped device.

The Crescent Device: This is the Dterrase. It is silver, with recessed connection ports and a few small controls. The entire device appears flawless and brand new. A character with any skill with the numenera can, without a roll, determine that this has something to do with the Uldada. But unless the characters have spoken with The Knowledge or found and examined the Abrustraithe in the Uldada, they cannot determine any other function or purpose.

If the Dterrase is removed from the Ancient Crèche and brought into the valley (or anywhere else), it alters the local weather conditions, stirring up an electrical storm in three to four hours. When the storm comes, the device is struck repeatedly by lightning.

Anyone touching the Dterrase when it is struck suffers 10 points of damage from the lightning. Anyone even within immediate range suffers 2 points of damage and is knocked down and stunned for 2 rounds, unable to take actions, if they fail a Might defense task (difficulty 4).

Once struck by lightning, the Dterrase can now function properly.

Uldada, page 93

The Knowledge, page 72

Dancer: *level 4, level 5 for Speed defense; immune to any energy attack; struck foes are thrown or knocked prone, and the next defense action the foe takes is hindered*

CHAPTER 8

KETTERACH

Aeon Priests, page 264

Jyrek, page 149

For more information about the Lands of the Dawn, see the Ninth World Guidebook.

Rising up at the entrance to the Glimmering Valley stand three tower like pillars of stone. This is Ketterach.

Over 6000 people live in Ketterach, although due to the nature of the city, the population is not obvious. The majority of the town is built within a trio of natural rock columns rising out of a lake formed by Loe's River, the core of this structure being a creation of the prior worlds. Nearby, a large bridge crosses the river, connecting to the even farther away isolated islands of civilization in the land of Thaemor.

Eventually, this road leads to the fortress-city of Jyrek to the south and west. Directly south, the road leads to what people call the Great Reach, which is a portal that leads to the so-called Lands of the Dawn on the far side of the continent. Thanks to these important locations, traffic along this road is heavy by Ninth World standards, bringing a lot of people and wealth to Ketterach.

Loe's River eventually flows into the much larger Wyr and from there goes to the sea (and Qi, the largest city in the Steadfast).

The entrance to the city is at the bottom of one of the three towers, reached by crossing a series of wide wooden rafts connected to form a floating bridge. When secured, this floating bridge can support a great deal of weight.

PEOPLE AND CULTURE

Compared to Neandran, Ketterach is much more akin to the people and cultures in the setting at large, as presented in *Numenera Discovery*. They're much more comfortable with the numenera and the concept of the prior worlds.

A small outpost of Aeon Priests in Ketterach serve the community and educate the locals in the ways of the Order of Truth. Through the priests and the traders that come and go on the road, the people of Ketterach know about the world, even though most have never left the confines of the town itself.

The people of Ketterach are aware of the lands beyond the valley—they have heard tell of the possibly insane king of Thaemor, and that beyond that land are others clustered together called the Steadfast. They know that the mountains to the east are called the Black Riage. But still, as with most people in the Ninth World, they haven't actually traveled there. Many are just as forever locked in Ketterach as the folk of Neandran are within their village. And the reason is mostly the same—travel is dangerous.

By Ninth World standards, Ketterach is a wealthy city. People's needs are met, most goods are readily available, and people have leisure time. People enjoy the competitions staged by the Parahawks in the skies above the city, as well as the output of the surprisingly active community of artists, musicians, and actors.

The people of the city are stratified into distinct classes, although even some among the lower class are well-off compared to the simple village folk of Neandran. Fashion

among the middle and upper classes is important, with stylishly dramatic and impractical garments being all the rage.

Unlike Neandran, crime is a real issue in Ketterach, including a few small but violent gangs operating within the city.

Because of the nature of the city, there are no individual houses or buildings. Everyone lives in private quarters of varying sizes, and generally speaking, the upper class lives in the highest portion of the city. Other buildings, like storehouses, shops, crafting workshops, and everything else are likewise located in chambers (or series of chambers) connected by the central corridors and stairways within the rock columns.

These connecting passages can seem odd, as they were not designed for humans. In places, they meander with twists and dead ends, creating little nooks. Sometimes criminals make use of these spots, but sometimes homeless people do as well. Some of the larger, more open spaces still hold synth sculptures from the original inhabitants of the city, but to human eyes they are abstract and—while pleasing—hold no meaning.

Fish and grain are food staples, and the city's breweries (located in the lower areas of the pillars) produce a wide variety of beers.

Religion is not very important to the majority of the population. There is a small chapel devoted to Loe, but it stands empty most of the time. A few other religions have shrines and so forth, but they are rare and out of the way.

AUTHORITIES

Red Gamesan serves as the mayor of Ketterach, chosen by select prominent citizens for a term of eight years. Gamesan prefers to be called "Red" due to a large reddish-purple birthmark that covers most of his face. He maintains a very relaxed, informal attitude most of the time, and has a remarkable memory for names. Most of the people of Ketterach believe themselves to be close friends of the mayor because of this welcoming, friendly nature. He is, however, also a very effective, very wise leader.

The mayor commands a small standing military force of only about thirty individuals. These people wear blue and silver uniforms of armoring cloth, and are typically armed with buzzers and broadswords. They also carry shields with a blue-and-silver hawk insignia. For the most part, they operate as a police force and their presence is heaviest in the Market and in the Outskirts.

Red Gamesan: *level 4; level 6 for pleasant social interaction, leadership, and memory*

Ketterach soldier: *level 3, level 4 for Speed defense due to shield; Armor 2*

Ketterach conscript: *level 2, level 3 for Speed defense due to shield; Armor 1*

Attela: *level 6, level 8 for paragliding, level 7 for attacking from above and Speed defense; health 26; Armor 1*

Parahawk: *level 4, level 6 for paragliding, level 5 for attacking from above and Speed defense; health 15; Armor 1*

Harrow hawk: *level 2, level 4 for Speed defense; can move a long distance in flight*

The trained harrow hawks show fierce loyalty. They can be employed as a falconer would—from a gloved hand—or they can accompany a paraglider through the air.

If need be, however, the city can put together a force of at least a thousand conscript soldiers. These people don't have uniforms, wear leather jerkins, and carry crossbows, spears, and shields. Should the city ever come under attack, however, the floating bridge spanning the lake can be quickly removed, shutting off the entrance to the city from the outside.

THE PARAHAWKS

An elite force of paragliders using their gliders to hunt, patrol, and defend the city, the Parahawks serve their leader, the Winglord. Each member has one or two trained harrow hawks that accompany them, helping find thermals to keep the paragliders aloft. Likewise, the birds serve as spotters for game on the ground, or other types of trouble, including fires or violence.

They can frequently be seen gliding around the columns of the city, launching from the highest terraces and balconies, or landing on those lower down.

The Winglord, Attela, is a harsh leader. Unlike the office of the mayor, the position of Winglord is a hereditary one, and she comes from a long tradition of imperious disciplinarians who accept only the best from their underlings. Her harsh treatment and demanding standards—and those of the Winglords before her—have given rise to an elitist, arrogant demeanor among the membership of the Parahawks.

The Parahawks consider themselves to be paragons nonpareil in Ketterach, lording their station above all others. Attela the Winglord sees even the mayor to be beneath her and, should it ever come to it, would attempt to oust him if he ever crossed her.

LOCATIONS IN KETTERACH

Ketterach has many locations, but these are the ones the PCs might find most interesting.

THE MARKET

The general marketplace of Ketterach offers a wide variety of goods. Folks from Neandran likely won't know what half of the wares are, since they've never seen them before. The city has far greater access to metal and synth, and a much greater variety of foodstuffs available. Most of the sellers are open to haggling. Likewise, they're open to cheating a naive out-of-towner.

While cyphers or artifacts can't really be purchased here, some iotum can. The PCs can get up to 3 units of responsive synth (3 shins each), 4 units of bio-circuitry (5 shins each), and 2 units of pliable metal (10 shins each). These merchants will also take io as currency (1 io = 1 shin).

THE CRYSTAL SHARD

There are a few bars in Ketterach, but the Crystal Shard is likely the most interesting (particularly to the PCs). It's named after the shard of crystal that hangs in a glass case in the center of the main taproom, and folks from Neandran recognize it immediately as a piece of one of the crystal monoliths in the village, although no one has ever heard of pieces breaking off.

The Crystal Shard caters to travelers, so characters can be exposed to all sorts of people from across the Steadfast (and maybe even the Lands of the Dawn). That means that many of them are traders, merchants, caravan guards, or adventurers. It also means that the PCs might see their first visitant, cyborg, or even an intelligent automaton.

The bar is run by a woman named Akel, a tall, thin, humorless woman with a head for business.

If one of the players wants to introduce a new character in Ketterach, taking advantage of the fact that any character option is open, having the other PCs meet the new character in the Crystal Shard perhaps makes sense.

Akel: *level 3, level 4 for seeing through deception and business*

Typical merchant: *level 2, level 4 for trickery and seeing through deception, level 3 for persuasion*

THE LIBRARY

The Aeon Priests maintain a substantive library in Ketterach. They do not loan out books, but allow anyone to read any of their volumes in the reading room.

Here in this library, people can discover information about the flora and fauna of the Glimmering Valley, generalities of science and the numenera, and the basics of a great many skills and areas of knowledge and interest. There's even some poetry and fiction.

Essatha, page 104

Only a little can be learned about Thaemor and a very little about the Steadfast. Most histories limit their coverage to events in and around Ketterach itself.

PCs from Neandran can find records of their own village dating back farther than any native of Neandran knows. According to these accounts, the village was first established almost 300 years ago, shortly after Ketterach itself. Those first villagers were mostly people who had no interest in living in the rocks of the city, and others who thought they could make a good living for themselves as hunters and trappers. Originally, the two settlements had far more contact than they do today, with many of the Neandran folk coming to Ketterach during the coldest part of the winter. Obviously, over the generations, this changed. For the last 100 years or so, Neandran has been an almost forgotten village in the deep, remote valley—a valley many consider too dangerous to traverse.

Convergence, page 216

The GM should decide whether or not to allow connections to the other magisters and magistrixes of the Convergence and what doing so would mean. It is outside the bounds of this book.

Empty Sanctum, page 172

Golden Sanctum, page 138

THE ORDER OF TRUTH

Near the Library is the outpost of the Aeon Priests in Ketterach. Compared to many locations in the Steadfast, the Order of Truth has not been in Ketterach long—only about ten years. In their enclave, the five Aeon Priests assigned to the city work at building devices that can benefit the city, often at the behest of Red Gamesan. The mayor reluctantly works with the priests, leery that they will usurp too much power in the city, but still willing to accept the conveniences they offer.

Just establishing themselves and earning the goodwill of the citizens has kept the Aeon Priests here busy (not helped by the fact that they have had a lot of personnel turnover, with priests being called away to other locations and then replaced). Their current goal is to establish a school so they can begin training new priests. They have not even begun to investigate the valley and whatever ancient wonders it might hold.

ESSATHA'S HOME

Essatha dwells in the upper portions of the city, being wealthy and a member of the upper class. She is not originally from Ketterach, but has maintained her home here for two years, intrigued by the ancient past of the valley (and what it can do for her).

Like most Ketterach residents, Essatha keeps her door locked. In her case, it's a conventional but upgraded lock (difficulty 5).

The home includes six rooms: a large, plush bedroom; a workshop; a sitting room (with a small dining area); a kitchen; a small bedroom; and a bathroom. The contents and furnishings of these rooms are of exquisite make and very valuable.

Her Bedroom: Perhaps not surprisingly, Essatha's personal chamber holds some secrets. Hidden behind the bedside table in the larger bedroom, a secret cache (difficulty 4 to find) holds a locked iron box (difficulty 5 to open). Inside is an artifact communicator. This level 3 device is made of glass and synth, covered in knobs and buttons. It must be adjusted to tune it to the proper frequency when used, but it allows Essatha to communicate with other members of the Convergence. It has a depletion of 1 in 1d100. With the device is a small notebook with names and numbers, these being other members that she knows that have similar devices, and the frequency used to communicate with them. These include entries for Mnoma, Iom, the Empty Sanctum, and the Golden Sanctum. The notebook's cover bears the symbol of the Convergence, an entwined eye.

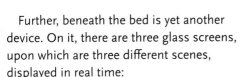

Further, beneath the bed is yet another device. On it, there are three glass screens, upon which are three different scenes, displayed in real time:

- The entrance to the Ancient Crèche
- The Haunted Stair
- Neandran, focusing on the growing Uldada

Essatha has secreted cameras in these places to keep tabs on them.

The Workshop: What the PCs are likely most interested in, however, is the workshop. The shop is the largest room and serves as a small library and study as well as an area in which Essatha can create and experiment. A variety of half-finished projects (cyphers, oddities, and so on) lie about on tables under mounted magnifying glasses or lamps. Tools sit in well-organized drawers and bins. The workshop is extremely tidy.

Amid the books and papers are two things very valuable to the PCs:

- Directions to The Knowledge in the Ancient Crèche. This is basically a drawing that shows the entrance in the Outer Cave, the Vertical Shaft, and at the top of the shaft the Rhombohedron. It says to hug the walls in the room with the Rhombohedron and get to the passage leading to the Sealed Barrier. It has the sequence used to open the barrier, and then directions to go through the Strobing Corridor to The Knowledge. It says topics to ask The Knowledge include the structure being built in the valley and the strider. No other information or details are provided in the directions.
- The plans for building a Dterrase.

Finding these things, however, is onerous because of the sheer volume of material. Essatha keeps detailed notes about a great many topics, and the vast majority of these are meaningless to the PCs. If they know exactly what they're looking for, it takes about an hour of searching to find one of the two important things, and a half hour to find the other. If they are searching randomly, this will take at least six times that long.

To someone who can use them, there are six other random numenera plans along with the Dterrase plan.

The workshop's other treasures include 25 units of parts, 20 units of io, 5 units of responsive synth, and 1 unit of amber crystal. And of course, the tools themselves are valuable to anyone working with the numenera.

SLEEPING LAKE

Sleeping Lake got its name from its very calm waters. So calm that a series of large, secured rafts compose a floating bridge that connects the shore of the lake to the base of one of the columns of the city where gates of ancient metal provide access inside.

Known by some as "Seeping Lake," the body of water around the pillars of Ketterach is relatively shallow, although those who know it know that there is actually a substantial flooded cave system beneath the lake—effectively a lake beneath a lake. This underground lake can be reached via an entrance at the lake bottom, near the base of the rock columns. Like the interior of the city itself, these caves were part of an ancient structure used in the prior worlds. Unlike the city, the submerged caves have not been fully explored or salvaged.

Becha is an explorer that combs the underground caves for ancient devices or parts—a lucrative business. She has built several diving suits with their own air supplies and protection against the cold. She can be convinced to sell (or in fact, trade) one or two to others who would like to perform some underwater exploration.

THE OUTSKIRTS

Around the lake, people have built homes and other structures, particularly near the bridge. This includes fishing wharfs, a few warehouses, a leather tannery, and an ironworks. There is also a tavern and a hostel for travelers who don't want to go all the way up into the city.

Ancient metal gates: *level 8*

Characters that want to explore the bottom of Lake Memory could certainly put one of Becha's suits to good use.

Ancient Crèche, page 61

Becha: *level 3, level 4 for swimming, diving, and resisting the effects of cold*

Becha's diving suits: *artifact level 3; provides air and 5 points of Armor against cold and pressure; depletion 1 in 1d10 (check each full hour of use)*

Dterrase plan, page 99

The outskirts are utterly destroyed when the ourach invasion begins.

CHARACTER CREATION IN KETTERACH

Once the PCs visit Ketterach, all options are available to newly created characters. A new character can choose any descriptor, type, and focus. Even a visitant character or other options are available if both GM and player agree.

Further, existing characters can switch their type to one of the *Destiny* types not available originally to inhabitants of their little village. This is important, because saving Neandran might very well require an Arkus, a Wright, or a Delve (perhaps in particular a Wright).

The transition here isn't about maximizing characters but instead about narrative. It should feel right in terms of the story. If this is the case, studying in the library in Ketterach or talking to like-minded folk there for even just a week might allow the transition to another type.

The easiest transitions (narratively speaking) would probably look something like this:

Type	Transition Options
Nano	Wright or Delve
Glaive	Arkus or Delve
Jack	Delve or Arkus

Truthfully, however, GMs should permit a character of any *Discovery* type to transition to any *Destiny* type if they really want to.

When a character changes their type, stat Pools and Edge do not change. Neither does starting equipment, nor weapon and armor use. Granting the character the skill that lies at the heart of each Type (the one they get for free at tier One) would not be unbalancing, however:

Arkus: Persuasion

Wright: Crafting numenera

Delve: Salvaging numenera

Most other changes won't be immediate—they won't take place until the character gains a new tier. However, on a case-by-case basis, the GM should allow a player who wishes to trade in old abilities for those of the new type even before the tier advancement occurs.

For example, a Nano who is going to transition into a Wright might decide to trade one of their tier 1 esoteries for a tier 1 inspired technique. So they might lose their Ward and gain Deconstruct.

When the character gains a new tier, they gain the abilities (or the choice of abilities) as described for the new type and the new tier. So our tier 1 Nano transitioning to Wright would be a tier 2 Wright, and would gain two numenera plans and an inspired technique.

Once the transition is made, the characters can go on to become something truly unique, particularly in the name of their village of origin. If the Glimmering Valley campaign is, at least in part, about saving Neandran, all three of the *Destiny* types have a special role to play in that endeavor.

CHAPTER 9

THE BRIINII

Not all the people of the valley are human.

The briinii discovered the valley about thirty years ago and now come back every winter. They are biomechanical beings of great intellect but mysterious disposition. This is their truth: their ancestors were technologically sophisticated, living a life of complexity and disharmony. They found that technology did not bring them a better existence—so they rejected much of it. The briinii of today live a simple life by choice. Their prior existence now lies so many generations in their past that they have all but forgotten it.

Briinii biomechanical nature, however, still grants them some interesting advantages when it comes to using or interacting with the numenera. When they touch virtually any powered advanced machine, tiny fibers extend from their flesh and connect them to it. With this connection, tasks to interact with the device are made simpler.

Thanks to their connection to technology that utilizes electricity or similar power sources, they can sense the flow of such energy. This enables them to both sense the presence of technology as well as technological connections. For example, they can use this to sense the connection between a radio and a receiver, and can identify which control panel operates a specific machine.

Further, their unique physiognomy gives them 1 Armor against any sort of damaging energy attack (fire, electricity, radiation, etc.).

It can be difficult for non-briinii to distinguish one individual from another, although briinii have no such difficulty. One reason is that the briinii are without the conventions of gender, as individuals are intersex. They are all both male and female. When two briinii want to have a child, they decide for themselves which will carry the child.

Briinii are hunters and craftspeople of great skill. Their ability to pass through the forest unseen and unheard rivals that of skilled hunters like Mert.

The briinii are aware of the Dream, and know that it is a transmission from somewhere, although they don't understand it any better than the humans of the valley. They can use their own biomechanical nature to "turn it off" for their own mind should they desire. Doing so means they just have "normal" dreams when they sleep.

Briinii use spears and long, slightly curved blades they call sesh. They wear leather armor of their own design studded with small bits of metal. There are about 200 briinii in the clan. Through necessity, only the very young or the very old are not considered warriors.

Ionea serves as the clan leader, and has for decades. Although briinii live extremely long lives by human standards, Ionea's best years lie behind them. They walk with a stoop and move slowly. But they have the love and respect of all the rest of the clan. Like all their people, Ionea has learned to be wary of humans (and all other intelligent species), but doing something helpful for the clan can change their mind. Personal gifts, flattery, or other typical ways of earning goodwill do not work with them.

Briinii: bri-IN-eye-ee

Mert, page 27

The Dream, page 10

The briinii very likely came, originally, from another world. This happened so long ago, however, that they have no memory of that (certainly not that they will share).

This puts them in a similar position of the settings "visitants," such as the varjellen and the lattimor presented in Numenera: Discovery. However, they do not have that term or that context, nor do the PCs.

Ui: oo-EE
Aria: ar-EE-uh

Iea: eye-EE-ah

Followers, page 17

Uldada, page 93

Ourach Invasion, page 100

BRIINII EVENTS

The briinii arrive in the valley and make their encampment probably three or four weeks after the start of the campaign. They've been coming to this same spot for a generation—the folks in Neandran know of them. The villagers know that the briinii aren't overly hostile, but they still fear them a little bit, as they're strangers in every sense of the word. When the briinii first started to winter in the Glimmering Valley, there were some bad moments, and blood was spilled on both sides. While that conflict was smoothed over before it got very far, the ripples in its wake are still felt down through the years and even today.

The briinii, likewise, have learned to steer clear of the humans. This is true in the valley and it's true in the other lands in which they travel.

The PCs might want to go investigate the camp once they hear that the briinii have arrived. Others in the village discourage this, but the characters can do as they wish. They find the briinii to be standoffish and cold. For the briinii clan, it's actions that matter, not words, and humans showing up at their camp, no matter how friendly, makes them nervous.

LOST BRIINII

A very young briinii named Iea gets lost looking for a cave they've heard others speak of. If they haven't come to the camp on their own, coming upon the lost child in the woods might be the PCs' first time meeting the briinii. Bringing Iea back to the camp earns the PCs a lot of goodwill.

BRIINII SPECIES DESCRIPTOR

Once the PCs have made allies of the briinii, players can opt to select the briinii species descriptor when bringing in a new character.

Briinii are typically Glaives or Jacks, although an Arkus is a possibility. A briinii Nano, Wright, or Delve would likely be an outcast, as such pursuits are not a part of their culture.

Tough: Briinii add 2 to their Might Pool.
Energy resilience: Briinii have 1 Armor against damaging energy attacks, including ambient dangers.
Machine adaptation: Briinii gain an asset to all tasks involving powered machines.
Reject technology: Cypher limit is reduced by 1.

A HARSH WINTER

During one of the snowstorms that come during the winter, hunting becomes difficult. Luttan in Neandran has prepared for this with a nice stockpile of food, but the briinii don't have big storehouses.

Should the PCs think of it and manage to pull it off, bringing food to the clan at this time would save lives.

The briinii may have a different value system than the humans (they don't think in terms of valuables, money, or such things), but they value food and survival. This endeavor on the PCs' part will earn them a great amount of respect and goodwill.

POTENTIAL ALLIES

Two of the younger members of the group, named Ui and Aria, are skeptical of the truths that many of the others believe in. They are intrigued by humans and interested in the ancient past. They might meet up with the PCs on a visit to the camp, or they might go looking for the "humans who aren't afraid to leave their village." They approach out of curiosity and potential friendship. They want to know what the PCs seek.

Ui and Aria offer to accompany the PCs if they find out the PCs are headed to the Ancient Crèche, as they're curious about that too. They don't have any information about it other than the fact that it exists. Treat both as level 2 followers, helping in any way that they can.

THE ULDADA

At some point, the PCs (or others from the village) might decide to come to the briinii for help with the growing structure that threatens Neandran. If some kind of good relationship has been established, the briinii will help, and their nature makes them keen allies in this endeavor. They have no foreknowledge of it, though. It's as new and strange to them as it is to the villagers.

THE OURACH

Should the ourach invade the forest and move toward Neandran, the briinii attempt to fight them off. PCs who have forged a good relationship with the briinii can coordinate the resistance against the invaders. It still might not be enough, but it's better than fighting alone.

CHAPTER 10

THE ULDADA

This chapter presents event-based adventure content for the Glimmering Valley. The temple and the crystal monoliths of Neandran are in fact a part of an ancient structure or complex of structures called the Uldada. The PCs have no way of knowing this at the start, but as they explore the Ancient Crèche or interact with Essatha in Ketterach, they can begin to pick up some information about the structure and how to stop it from destroying the village.

It's probably worth stating that, as this is a prior-world creation, it's impossible to comprehend what the Uldada truly is, and what it will do if it grows to completion. Likely, it does something on a scale so massive that the people of the valley couldn't see it happen, like communicate with some distant civilization across the galaxy, alter some quantum process in reality, or slightly change the climate over the next million years. Just as likely, conditions or the status of other machines it would interact with have changed so much that it ultimately does . . . nothing. Does the civilization across the galaxy still exist? Does the machine that it worked with to change the quantum process still function? Do the climate conditions that it alters have any effect anymore? Even if the PCs learned which of these questions is relevant (if any) and also learned the answer to the question, it would be meaningless to them.

In short, then, let the players ponder and muse about what the structure growing in Neandran does, but its function isn't the point. What's truly relevant to their characters is that it is going to destroy the village that they have lived in their whole lives and all their friends and family are in danger.

THE BEGINNING

Soon after the campaign is in swing, but not before the players have had a chance to get their bearings and do a few things—perhaps in the second session—reports of strange things begin to come from across the village.

- **Strange sounds:** Rumblings, not unlike an upset, gurgling stomach, rise from beneath the surface. This is the first thing that people notice, but they continue throughout the entire process.
- **Sinkholes:** Sinkholes form as the ground collapses: one to the south of the eastern storehouse and another just south of the western thates fields. Next, in the center of the village, another even larger sinkhole opens up, this time right beneath the feet of Aryle, who breaks his leg in the fall and needs to be rescued from the 12-foot (4 m) deep pit.
- **Objects push up from underground:** With colossal thrusts not unlike powerfully wielded swords, long metal beams emerge from the ground, some rising 8 feet (2.5 m) from the surface. These beams are 6 inches (15 cm) thick.

Neandran, page 22

Ancient Crèche, page 61

Essatha, page 104

Ketterach, page 84

Of all the event-based adventure material, "The Uldada" asks that you keep fairly close track of the passage of time in the campaign.

It's important that unless the PCs learn the name "Uldada" by interacting with The Knowledge in the Ancient Crèche (page 61) or from Essatha (page 104) or possibly from a glimmer (page 12) no one in Neandran will actually use that term. Instead, they will use the term from the dream, the "growing forest."

Aryle, page 24

Support beams: *level 9*

The names involved with the Uldada, such as Dterrase and Naracodium, are meant to be alien-sounding and strange. If the players are really struggling with them, you can use the alternative names, "Kill Switch" and "Reversal Switch" at the table much of the time.

THE PROGRESSION

A clear pattern forms over the weeks to follow. A structure slowly constructs itself on the site of the village. This process will undoubtedly destroy Neandran. The exact time the construction will take is unclear (at least at first), but there are three stages of its progress after it begins, and someone with some knowledge of the numenera (difficulty 4) can determine what stage is currently happening and how many stages are left.

Easchel, page 24

The best way to measure the progression is by matching it to the PCs' tier, but don't tell the players that. You don't want them to feel punished for advancing. Maybe don't match the progression precisely, but generally speaking, the Uldada's construction should last for however long it takes for the PCs to reach tier 3. Unless they stop it, of course.

Amrose, page 23

However, speaking of matters escalating, it's also important to make it clear to the PCs that the progression is taking place. Each return to Neandran should always reveal differences that occurred while they were gone. Even in the course of one day, PCs looking for them should see differences, much like noticing changes amid the construction of a building that you see every day in the real world. If the PCs are gone for quite a while, the changes should be dramatic.

Sesson, page 28

Sesson

STAGE ONE (TIER 1): 1–6 WEEKS

At first, the metal beams continue to rise from the ground a few inches each day. The rumbling sounds grow louder. Another sinkhole opens up beneath a villager's home, swallowing it.

The people of Neandran gather in a meeting involving almost everyone in the village to discuss what to do. Some people suggest going to Ketterach for help, but this is not popular. Easchel dominates a part of the meeting while he warns of the dangers of sorcery and how these events are just proof that he's been right all along. Sesson calmly presses for faith in the mercy of Loe to take care of them. Amrose suggests waiting to see what happens since no one among the villagers knows anything about what's going on.

If the PCs attend this meeting, they are free to contribute suggestions and ideas, but unless they succeed at a level 6 task to influence and persuade, their opinions won't carry much weight compared to the older, more trusted residents. Thus, the most likely outcome of this meeting is nothing.

If the PCs are known "adventurous spirits," however, someone—depending on their relationships with people in the village—might very well quietly suggest that they explore the valley and see if anything else strange is going on, and if there's possibly anything that can be done.

At the end of Stage One, a platform beneath the temple rises upward, elevating the structure a few inches above the ground. The platform is 60 feet (20 m) wide on each side, and the temple is affixed to it, as though it was always that way. Sesson assures everyone that the temple is safe and continues to conduct ceremonies there as he always has.

(It will seem as if the platform was always beneath the temple and is now simply rising from below the surface. It may not be important, but that isn't entirely true—the platform is being built by the Uldada process, molecule by molecule, which is raising the platform.)

STAGE TWO (TIER 2): 7–10 WEEKS

More, larger support structures thrust up from underground. Foundational reinforcements grow as if built by invisible hands (these are nanotech machines literally transforming the air and ground to building materials on a molecular level). One of the western storehouses and Jofan's house are destroyed by the sudden appearance of the new pylons and supports. The animals are terrified, and the gobrin begin giving less milk. People are, at best, worried, and at worst have fully panicked. Many are relocating to hastily built shelters in the wood, at least a quarter mile from the village, but this causes hardship as the cold weather has set in, as well as the rain and even some snow.

PCs that can provide any aid or assistance to people are noticed and appreciated. It will continue to raise people's opinions of them, and earn them more trust.

The temple, now on a still-rising platform, is 5 feet (1.5 m) higher than it used to be. Sesson insists on retaining access to it and uses a wooden ladder to get to it.

Toward the very end of this stage, the toothed eye is loose and looking for the Uldada. It doesn't find it until well into Stage Three.

STAGE THREE (TIER 3): 11-16 WEEKS

There are still spaces between the rising pylons and support structures that seem mostly safe if people remain in the village, but the constant noises and occasional shaking of the ground make it a strange place to be. Most of the residents have moved out of the village, at least temporarily.

During this stage, however, the beginnings of an entirely new structure rise beneath Luttan's house. A week later, a similar thing happens at the site of Kyath's house.

Foul smells rise from cracks in the earth. The temple is now unreachable, as it forms the top of the central Uldada structure, which is now 20 feet (6 m) in the air (and rising).

The Post collapses. More and more of the village is completely uninhabitable. The gobrin stop producing milk entirely.

At the end of this stage, the structure is complete.

Jofan, page 26

Luttan, page 26

Kyath, page 26

The Post, page 30

Sometimes strict time-based adventures can cause problems—even with the 2-5 week variations built into the stages. Creating a great story that is fun relies heavily on timing, and a strict timetable can make that difficult, depending on your GMing style and the group's preferred type of play.

For example, if the group likes to do only a few things in a given day and moves slowly through encounters, the Uldada might progress far too quickly. Conversely, if the group likes to pack a lot of action into a single day, not much actual time will pass and the PCs will advance very quickly. That's why matching the progression with PC tier might be best.

WHAT THE VILLAGERS DO

The people of the village can pack up and leave, relocating somewhere else in the valley, but are obviously reluctant to do so. First and foremost, the village is the only home they've ever known. Further, it's built in the perfect location to meet all of the villagers' needs. The wisest of residents—including Amrose, Luttan, and Kyath—strongly suspect that the crystal monoliths contribute greatly to the fertility of the soil and the success of the flocks. Last but not least, the temple is important to the villagers. Many have always seen the location of the village as a gift from Loe themselves, and abandoning the Crystal Monolith would show a lack of faith or gratitude.

Meanwhile Illace and her fellow cultists see the Uldada as a sign of the Uttarek's ascendency and prepare for their secret masters' arrival and rewards. As such, they will act against anyone who has a potential legitimate solution to stop the Uldada.

By the time the Uldada progresses to Stage Three, however, leaving the village really is no longer a debatable point. The entire site of Neandran will be destroyed from below.

If the village is destroyed, Sesson leads the villagers in fervent, heartfelt pleas to Loe for mercy and salvation. Amrose tries to organize a mass exodus to Ketterach, while Easchel argues against it (although he has no alternative solution).

THE FINALE AND THE FINISHED STRUCTURE

If it's not stopped, the Uldada will destroy Neandran. Anyone remaining in the village in the last few weeks of the Uldada's progression will be lost.

The completed Uldada is a towering edifice of irregular shape, seemingly comprised by at least seven different structures compacted together so closely that the complex could be thought of as just a single building. Like nothing a human would ever build, it is made of gleaming silver-and-red metal, much stronger than steel. The sounds of brand-new machinery waft forth, whirring and humming with a life all their own.

Essatha, page 104

Neandran is gone, and its residents are driven off. The flora of the surrounding woods begins to wither slowly, over time. The River Loe, as it passes near the Uldada, grows murky with a faintly orange cast. Fish die. Plants along the riverbanks die. Eventually, people from Ketterach come to investigate (but likely can do nothing).

Toothed Eye, page 117

ESSATHA

Just as the Uldada Process (the "Process") completes, Essatha and her followers arrive in the area (assuming that she and they are still alive). This is her moment of triumph, for she has crafted an artifact that allows her to enter the Uldada by creating a large door in the side, where no door had existed before. Glimpses through the door reveal a location that can only be understood as *somewhere else*. She passes through and closes the door and is very likely never seen on Earth again. Did she travel to another world? Another time? Another state of reality? No way to tell. But presumably, in so doing she amasses power, knowledge, or both.

If the PCs are present, Essatha will fight if she needs to create the door and get through. Her assistants aid her, but in the end, she doesn't give them the opportunity to get through.

If the toothed eye is present, it may in fact attack anyone approaching the Uldada if given a chance. (If Essatha opens the door and moves through it quickly, it won't have the chance to attack her.)

THE TOOTHED EYE APPEARS

If it's not intercepted, the toothed eye arrives in Neandran during Stage Three. It sets itself up as a guardian of the Uldada, and the Abrustraithe in particular. It does not allow anyone near the Abrustraithe and defends it to the death. In the long term, it begins to prey on the people that might remain after the completion of the Uldada, becoming a menace to the entire area.

STOPPING THE ULDADA

Characters with knowledge of the numenera are crucial in saving the village, and most villagers become certain that the means of stopping the coming disaster must lie in the knowledge of the prior worlds.

Obviously, Easchel opposes any attempt to use the numenera, even to deal with this issue, and heated arguments split the villagers (with only a vocal minority on Easchel's side).

Illace vocally supports Easchel in this, not because she actually agrees with him but because she believes that the Uldada is the work of the gods she secretly worships and thus it should not be stopped.

EXPLORING, LEARNING, AND SALVAGING

You fight fire with fire and you fight the numenera with numenera. The most straightforward means of stopping the Uldada from destroying Neandran is by using the numenera to essentially turn it off, or even destroy it.

Even this straightforward approach, however, involves exploring ancient ruins for information or learning from Essatha in Ketterach (or both). It involves salvaging valuable components from ancient devices to build or modify what they need. It may be the most direct solution, but it is not *easy*.

The Ancient Crèche: The real key(s) to stopping the Uldada lies in the Ancient Crèche. If the PCs speak with The Knowledge, they can learn about the following:

- The Abrustraithe: This is a portion of the Uldada that will form at the end of Stage Two of the structure's development. It is vital to the continuing growth of the structure. Think of it as the heart of the Uldada. It resembles an upright lozenge that is *vell* in color.

- The Dterrase: This is a tool that can be used to deactivate the Abrustraithe. Think of it as a sort of "kill switch" that can stop the heart. Keep in mind, however, that it is possible to reactivate the Abrustraithe using the Dterrase as well. It's a switch that can turn the Uldada off, but also back on.

- The Naracodium: This is a device that can literally cause the Uldada to discorporate and recede back into the ground, effectively undoing its appearance and restoring the area (that is to say, Neandran). Think of it as the "reversal switch." It is currently nonfunctional, but it could be rebuilt.

Essatha: It's possible that the PCs could discover details about The Knowledge (in the Ancient Crèche) from Essatha in Ketterach. She knows how to get to and interact with it, and she has also recorded the details in a file in her home. Her home also contains the plans for crafting her own Dterrase.

She will not tell the PCs about the Naracodium in any event, because its actions cannot be undone as far as she knows. But she might divulge information about the Dterrase in the Ancient Crèche if she must because she knows how to reactivate the Abrustraithe if she wants to (with her own Dterrase).

Thus, if she's not stopped, even if the PCs stop the Uldada by deactivating the Abrustraithe, she will come to Neandran and reactivate it. She wants it completed and won't stop until it is, or until she's dead.

APPEALING TO THE BRIINII

It's possible that the PCs (or someone else in the village) might believe that the briinii can help. The very thing that makes so many people afraid of them is what is needed now—an affinity with the numenera and the prior worlds.

Indeed, the briinii can be of help, but only if someone (likely the PCs) forms a very good relationship with them. If this is the case, Ionea, the leader, sends one or two of their people back to Neandran with the individuals that came asking for help.

The briinii don't possess any prior knowledge of the Uldada. They can, however, sense its connection with both the dream and the Ancient Crèche (a place they know of but diligently avoid).

Because of their fibrous connection to numenera, working with even just one briinii eases any task involving the Uldada by 2 steps.

Easchel, page 24

The Knowledge, page 72
Illace, page 25
The Ancient Crèche, page 61

Ketterach, page 84

Dterrase, page 99

Naracodium, page 80

Briinii, page 91

OTHER POSSIBLE SOLUTIONS (THAT ALMOST CERTAINLY FAIL)

Physically damaging the structure is not the answer. Even if a support beam here or a wall panel there is cut, pried away, or destroyed, the Uldada repairs the damage overnight.

Digging down to try to get at the foundation or the source of the structural pieces doesn't work either. Despite the appearances, the Uldada isn't actually coming up from beneath the ground. Rather, it is being created on a molecular level by nanotechnology.

Going to Ketterach for help isn't a bad plan, but it very likely won't work because by the time the PCs reach that city, the ourach invasion has already begun and the people of that city—and in particular the Aeon Priests there—have their own problems without having to also worry about a tiny village so far away.

SOMETHING ELSE

It wouldn't be a roleplaying game if only the Dterrase can stop the Uldada. Players come up with all sorts of inspired ideas, and Numenera offers characters a wide range of abilities. If the PCs attempt something not listed here that seems like it might work, let them try. But keep the following in mind:

- It should be difficult.
- It should involve multiple steps.
- There should be some element of danger or other serious risk.
- There should be some sort of cost.

GM intrusion: While in Neandran after the Uldada has begun to emerge, a character is much too close to a small sinkhole that opens suddenly, and without a successful Speed defense roll (difficulty 4), the character falls into it, suffering 4 points of damage and getting trapped amid the fallen earth.

Illace and the cultists, page 25

USING THE DTERRASE (THE KILL SWITCH)

The Dterrase must be hooked into the Abrustraithe, which means that the Abrustraithe must be located first. This cannot even be attempted before the last week or so of Stage Two, as the Abrustraithe isn't completed until then. Locating it requires a successful understanding numenera task with a difficulty of 6. Possessing the Dterrase is an asset for this roll. PCs must enter and ascend the interior of the structure to find the Abrustraithe, which is currently near the center of the structure.

Once it is located, a connection must be fashioned so that the Dterrase can communicate with the heart. This requires 12 units of bio-circuitry, 12 units of parts, and a successful crafting numenera task with a difficulty of 4.

Lastly, utilizing the Dterrase as a kill switch is a difficulty 4 understanding numenera task. Smart characters will remove the Dterrase once they've activated it because anyone could potentially use it to start the Process again.

- Find the Abrustraithe inside the structure (understanding numenera difficulty 6)
- Connect the Dterrase, found in the Ancient Crèche (crafting numenera difficulty 4 plus some iotum and parts)
- Activate the Dterrase (understanding numenera difficulty 4)

ILLACE'S INTERFERENCE

Unless the PCs keep this plan a secret, if they obtain the Dterrase—the most obvious possible solution—this will provoke Illace and her fellow cultists to act. Since they see the Uldada's creation as a sign from their gods, they interfere by attempting to steal the Dterrase. Keeping their identities a secret is very important to them, however, so they might try multiple times, fleeing before they get caught. If that doesn't work, the desperate cultists will try to destroy or damage the Dterrase, armed with knives and hammers. Doing so overtly will probably reveal their identities. They aren't murderous, however, so they won't attack the PCs—although they will fight in self-defense.

BUILDING A NEW DTERRASE FROM SCRATCH

A character that has examined the Dterrase has a chance to build one from scratch if they must. This could happen if either Illace or Essatha steals or destroys the device.

The Dterrase is a level 3 "installation." The difficulty for crafting it would then be 5 (+2 for its being an installation) and the process would require two weeks of intensive work with a total of five tasks during that period (difficulty 1, difficulty 2, difficulty 3, difficulty 4, and finally difficulty 5). Without a plan, however, each task is also hindered. The crafting numenera skill reduces not just the difficulty but the time and number of successful tasks required, as described in *Numenera Destiny*.

Should they have the plans from Essatha's home in Ketterach, then the character faces no hindrance. They also need not have seen the Dterrase in the Ancient Crèche in order to use the plans.

DTERRASE PLAN

Minimum Crafting Level: 3
Kind: Installation
Iotum: Io (1d6 units); bio-circuitry (20 units); pliable metal (2 units); mimetic gel (2 units); responsive synth (2 units)
Parts: 30 units
Specifications: This plan produces a crescent-shaped device with recessed connection ports and a few small controls. It can be used as a kill switch to stop the progression of the Uldada if properly connected. When first created, the device alters local weather conditions, stirring up an electrical storm in three to four hours. When the storm comes, the device is struck repeatedly by lightning. Anyone touching the Dterrase when it is struck suffers 10 points of damage from the lightning. Anyone even within an immediate range suffers 2 points of damage and is knocked down and stunned for 2 rounds, unable to take actions, if they fail a Might defense task (difficulty 4).
A character can use the Dterrase only after it is struck by lightning.
Depletion: —

REBUILDING THE NARACODIUM (THE REVERSAL SWITCH)

A character that has examined the Naracodium in the Ancient Crèche has a chance to rebuild it. This will take a very long time, however—in order for it to be completed before the village is destroyed, the character's crafting skill, if any, could speed up the process. Even reducing the difficulty by 1 step would turn the required three months into just one month.

Building the Naracodium is the most difficult and drastic solution to dealing with the Uldada, but it achieves by far the best and most satisfying results. However, characters who cannot do this in time should not be seen as failures.

THE NARACODIUM

The Naracodium is a level 5 "installation." The difficulty for crafting it would then be 7 (+2 for its being an installation) and the process would require three months of intensive work with a total of seven tasks during that period (difficulty 1, difficulty 2, difficulty 3, difficulty 4, difficulty 5, difficulty 6, and finally difficulty 7). Without a plan, however, each task is also hindered. The crafting numenera skill reduces not just the difficulty but the time and number of successful tasks required, as described in *Numenera Destiny*.

NARACODIUM PLAN

Minimum Crafting Level: 5
Kind: Installation
Iotum: Io (1d6 units); bio-circuitry (10 units); pliable metal (4 units); mimetic gel (4 units); responsive synth (4 units); kaon dot (1 unit)
Parts: 20 units
Specifications: This plan produces a metallic device that weighs about 70 pounds (30 kg) and is about the size of a person's leg. If attached to the Abrustraithe, it can cause the Uldada to discorporate and recede back into the ground, effectively undoing its appearance and restoring the area.
No actual crafting plan for the Naracodium exists in the valley. The PCs must craft it without a plan.
Depletion: Automatic

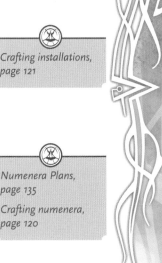

Crafting installations, page 121

Numenera Plans, page 135
Crafting numenera, page 120

CHAPTER
11

THE OURACH INVASION

Ourachs are monstrous abhumans that arrive in the Glimmering Valley once the campaign is underway. No one in Neandran has ever seen them before and even in Ketterach they are unknown—until they attack.

THE NATURE OF THE OURACHS

Like most abhumans, ourachs disdain most of the desirable aspects of humanity. They are bestial, cruel, selfish, and violent.

Cruelty and violence are particularly honed concepts for the ourachs. While they do not feed on fear, the smell of fear chemicals—and especially human fear chemicals—gives them great pleasure. It is both intoxicating and addicting for them. Their drive to terrorize others stands paramount to all other desires.

APPEARANCE

Ourachs have avian heads with sharp beaks, and two bony spikes that jut out from their backs. Their broad chests contrast with their thin, angular limbs. Despite having an avian look, they do not have feathers, and the hair on their bodies would more likely be thought of as quills.

The adornment of their back spikes indicates their success in battle and in spreading fear. They affix trophies, colored streamers, and other objects to them, even hammering in metal spikes.

Ourachs prefer to wear clothing of yellow or orange and strive to keep their garments more or less clean, working on doing so each night before sleep. The colors attest to their utter disregard for stealth. They do not sneak up on foes, nor do they set ambushes. They prefer brute force, the strength of numbers, and the momentum of utter savagery.

These abhumans craft armor from the carved and etched bones of their past victims. They likewise use javelins of bone and wood to attack at range or while mounted. In close quarters, however, they disdain weapons and use their natural claws and beaks.

CULTURE (SUCH AS IT IS)

Like most abhumans, ourachs base leadership on strength and ferocity. However, the power of these forceful leaders does not come from intimidation of their fellows, but rather respect. A strong ourach's position seems to simply be understood. The underlings don't act out of fear of their leaders, but rather out of the knowledge that a strong leader benefits them all and gets them what they all want.

Ourachs speak the Truth with gravelly voices. They do not have their own language, nor do they read or write. However, images—both decorative and representational—hold importance to them. They do not sing, as such, but they do howl. Their deep-throated bellows, done in unison when launching into battle or celebrating, inspire them and terrorize foes.

COMPANIONS

Unlike many abhumans, ourachs have domesticated—or perhaps a better word in this case might be dominated—other creatures. Specifically, they ride swift, long-legged mounts called cormentals and use attack hounds called corenda. The similar names of the two beasts are indicative of their symbiotic nature. Corenda latch themselves to the undersides of the cormentals with extremely flexible, six-jointed limbs. At a moment's notice— even if the cormentals are in motion—the corenda can detach and move into attack.

OUTLOOK AND MOTIVATION

Ourachs are merciless conquerors that lay waste to a region and then move on. The terror they crave is best when "fresh."

They do not take failure or their own fear well. This doesn't mean they fight to the death in every engagement, but it does mean they don't plan for retreat and don't even really comprehend the possibility of surrender. They don't go into an engagement with a Plan B. If they are driven back or routed in battle, it takes them time to regain themselves and comprehend (or intentionally forget) what just happened. If they come upon a challenge they cannot overcome in their first attempt, it takes them twice as long as one might expect to recover and adapt.

The ourach mind, then, does not dwell on either the past or the future. They are focused entirely on the present, and are stymied when it does not proceed as they expect.

Although they relish fear, they don't have the proper outlook to "farm" it. They might benefit from a slow campaign of terror or even from taking captives to terrorize over time, but they do neither. There are always new lands and new humans to conquer somewhere else.

OURACHS IN THE VALLEY

Their arrival in the relatively peaceful—sleepy, even—Glimmering Valley just at this moment is not a coincidence. They have been lured here by a figure in Ketterach named Essatha.

Eager for a new conquest, the ourachs gathered their horde and charged into the valley. Of course, the first place they came to was Ketterach, and they launched their attack. When the attack failed to gain access to the city, they set up camp and also sent a scouting party deeper into the valley.

Essatha, page 104

FIRST PC ENCOUNTER

The PCs first encounter a small scouting party of ourachs somewhere in the woods once they are closer to Ketterach than to Neandran. When this happens depends on how long it's taken the PCs to get to that part of the valley. It can't happen before the Uldada begins to form, and ideally well after that.

Ourach scouts, page 48

Uldada, page 93

ATTACK ON KETTERACH

Initially, the invading horde of ouarchs decimated all the structures around Sleeping Lake, including everything the people of Ketterach call the Outskirts. Before they could reach the floating bridge, however, the defenders were able to pull much of it into the city and let the other portions float away.

The main forces of ourachs lie in two encampments outside Ketterach, stymied by their utter failure to get to the main portion of the city. They slaughtered the poor souls that were unable to get to the safety of the upper city and now wait confoundedly, anxiously for a new plan. Ourachs are not stupid; they *will* come up with a renewed strategy, but it takes them a while.

Thus, by the time the PCs arrive, the initial battle is over, and it's now a quiet siege.

Each of the camps holds nearly a thousand abhumans, and three hundred mounts. While those numbers are fewer than the number of people in Ketterach, they are far larger than the number of able-bodied glaives the city can muster.

GETTING THROUGH THE SIEGE

When the PCs arrive, they see the two ourach camps and the decimated buildings around the lake. It's obvious what's going on. Assuming they are a small band and try to use a little stealth and caution, the characters can get inside the city with just a little ingenuity. While there are ourachs about, patrolling around the lake, it's merely a difficulty 3 task to sneak by and reach the shore. From there, they can use a small section of the cast-off floating bridge to float across the water, or they can simply swim. Either way, soldiers watch the entrance from within the city and open the gate if they see non-ourachs approach. Once the characters are in or on the water, the ourachs do not interfere even if they spot the PCs There's not much reason for the abhumans to care if someone is sneaking into the city, and they aren't good with the unexpected anyway.

It's also possible that one of Essatha's assistants—Malothy—will be on hand to help the PCs get into the city.

Inside, soldiers ask the characters what they saw, where they came from, and any other pertinent information they might have.

THE ONGOING CONFLICT

Meanwhile, the humans inside debate what they should do. Many hold the position that the city can simply wait. But with the city surrounded and few if any people getting in or out, food supplies will eventually begin to dwindle. From the city's position in the lake, some fishing and some gathering of resources are possible, but not enough to feed a city of six thousand people.

If the defenders do nothing, eventually, the ourachs will try to mount an assault by constructing crude rafts or even just swimming across the water. This will be very difficult and they probably won't succeed. But they still maintain their perimeter encircling the city to hold the siege.

PC ACTIONS

Of course, the PCs don't have to care what happens to Ketterach. It's not their home, and frankly few in the city would blame the characters if they left and went back to the village.

However, even slightly altruistic characters may offer to help in some way. If nothing else, they should realize that if Ketterach falls, Neandran will suffer—or it might be next.

PC-led sorties out from the city can harass the ourachs, but it's very unlikely minor attacks like this will drive off the abhumans.

The PCs might think to challenge the leader of the invading horde to a single combat. The ouarchs will not accept such a challenge—not out of fear, but because they have nothing to prove. They *want* to defeat Ketterach in battle, murdering the citizens and destroying the city completely. That's what they do, and what they hunger for.

However, if the PCs locate and defeat the leader without issuing any sort of challenge, there is a chance that it would have a profound effect. Since ourach society is based on respect, if the PCs destroy the leader quickly, decisively, and publicly, the invaders might decide to leave. Without their most respected leader and tactician, they might feel the need to retreat. Unfortunately, the invaders would return eventually with a new leader, and they might come with a way to get within the city, such as boats.

As the residents within the besieged city begin to starve, some will attempt to surrender to the ourachs, exiting from the city. The ourach don't take prisoners.

Leader of the horde: level 6, attacks level 7 when mounted, all actions level 4 if confused or routed; 22 health; 2 Armor

Help Getting In, page 105

KETTERACH'S DESPERATE PLAN

The Aeon Priests are building a bomb.

The bomb is designed to initially explode and fill a medium area, then scatter smaller bombs all around for a second series of explosions.

The plan is to detonate the bomb in the middle of the southern encampment, causing fear and confusion, and then launch an attack on the eastern camp with Ketterach's full force using a newly assembled floating bridge from inside the city's gates, hurriedly pushed out into the water and secured. The bomb is to be delivered from the air via the Parahawks. The ourachs, tightly packed into their encampment, will suffer heavy losses and won't react well to the shock and surprise.

If the PCs are present, they will be highly encouraged to join that full force. Rather than play out the entire battle, the GM can have the characters face off against 8–10 ourachs. The success of the PCs' battle is then mirrored in the larger battle. It's likely that the city's sortie is costly, but ultimately successful. The abhumans are routed and leave the valley angry and frustrated, their numbers greatly diminished.

Should the PCs' encounter go poorly, it is reflected in the success of the whole endeavor. The defenders will have to retreat back into the city. Some of the attacking horde gets inside the lower portions of the rock columns, although the defenses they meet inside likely drive them off. Losses on the defenders' side are heavy, and there is likely neither the will nor the capability to launch another counterattack.

THE AFTERMATH

If the defenders win, after the horde is gone, the dead need to be identified and buried. The destroyed Outskirts buildings need to be rebuilt. It is a time of mourning, and all of Ketterach is a strange mixture of elation and sadness.

If the defenders cannot drive off the ourach horde, they are trapped there unless someone else (the PCs?) can come up with a new plan. A few small groups might be able to sneak out of the city, but not long after, the abhumans put up an effective perimeter to keep anyone from escaping. A long, slow death from starvation and disease awaits the inhabitants of Ketterach, after which, if the scouts the horde sent into the valley report the existence of Neandran, the ourachs move against them next, burning the forest and scouring the valley. It's grim.

Attela: *level 6, level 8 for paragliding, level 7 for attacking from above and Speed defense; health 26; Armor 1*

Ketterach soldier: *level 3, level 4 for Speed defense due to shield; Armor 2*

Ketterach conscript: *level 2, level 3 for Speed defense due to shield; Armor 1*

Parahawk: *level 4, level 6 for paragliding, level 5 for attacking from above and Speed defense; health 15; Armor 1*

Harrow hawk: *level 2, level 4 for Speed defense; can move a long distance in flight*

CHAPTER

12

ESSATHA

Convergence, page 216

Essatha: *level 6; level 8 for numenera (understanding and crafting), level 7 for deception; health 28; Armor 3; can move fully out of phase for up to three rounds, project bolts of pure force up to very long range (inflicting 6 damage), and create level 6 walls and shapes filling an immediate area from pure force*

Essatha used her technical skills to wipe The Knowledge's memory of her.

Gravity detonation, page 277

The Dterrase is a crescent-shaped device with recessed connection ports and a few small controls. It can be used to stop (or start) the Uldudu Process. For more information, see page 97.

One more obstacle lies in the PCs' path, and that is a nano named Essatha. Essatha is a member of a very loose organization called the Convergence. These scattered nanos, tinkerers, and numenera experts study the secrets of the prior worlds, hoping to amass power for themselves and use their group connections to trade in information, technology, and ideas.

Essatha came to the Glimmering Valley because she wanted to know more about the prior-worlds structures there. She is smart, thorough, and extremely skilled in all things numenera. As such, she understands a bit more of the dream than anyone else. She knows it's a broadcast, and she knows that it signals the coming of the Uldada. She even has an idea of what the Uldada could be used for, if not its original purpose. Essatha has been to the Ancient Crèche, and has interacted with The Knowledge there. She's even built her own Dterrase to help control the Uldada. She may not be pulling all of the strings behind the scenes, but she is masterfully exploiting them.

Essatha's ruthlessness and determination surpass even her considerable knowledge of the ancient past and its wonders. To her, human connection pales in comparison to true knowledge and understanding, so things like ethics, loyalty, and compassion have no place in her plans. She only pretends to value or possess such qualities

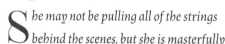

She may not be pulling all of the strings behind the scenes, but she is masterfully exploiting them.

to help her reach her goals, but she understands such things enough to use them to her advantage. She is a psychopath in the truest sense of the word.

Tall and lithe, Essatha smokes long cigarettes and wears dramatic and stylish clothing, in the manner of the upper classes of Ketterach. She has, however, modified herself to the point that she is clearly no longer fully human. Essatha's body (and brain) is more machine than flesh. Her hands and arms are metal (and full of devices). Most prominently, the upper half of her head (where a human's brain would be) is gone, replaced with a broad, flat, metal plate that is razor sharp. (Her brain is now located in her chest.) She enjoys having an appearance that is shocking and off-putting, and uses it to her advantage whenever she can.

In addition to the powers she gains from the devices built into her arms, she carries an artifact she calls the demoralizer, and two cyphers: a false fingertip with a reservoir of level 8 mind-controlling poison (victim obeys next verbal command given) and a level 8 gravity detonation. She also has her own, newly created Dterrase.

THE DEMORALIZER
Level: 6
Form: Spiky handheld device of synth with a single switch
Effect: All living beings within short range must succeed at an Intellect defense roll or become so dejected and hopeless that all actions are hindered by 2 steps for one round, and 1 step the following round.
Depletion: 1 in 1d10

INTERACTING WITH THE PCs

The characters draw Essatha's attention if they do any of the following:

- Enter the Ancient Crèche
- Enter the chambers below the Haunted Stair
- Thoroughly investigate the Uldada

After that point, she tries to keep an eye on them, probably by sending one or both of her assistants to spy on them occasionally.

A SPY

The first interaction the PCs will have with Essatha is a "coincidental" meeting with Nyka, her assistant. While moving from one place to another, the PCs encounter Nyka on a forest path. Nyka's there to get information and join with the PCs wherever they are going, if possible.

HELP GETTING IN

When the PCs arrive at Ketterach, it's under siege. Malothy, another of Essatha's assistants, hides outside of Ketterach, waiting for the PCs and keeping clear of the ourach patrols. He claims to be a resident of the city and he's got an idea of how to get in, but he needs help. He's neither charming nor persuasive, but he does his best and most of what he's saying is actually true. His plan is simple: sneak to where the floating bridge remnants are on the shore and use one as a raft to get to the city gates, where hopefully they'll be let in.

It's possible that Nyka is with the PCs when they arrive in Ketterach, and thus *both* of Essatha's people are with them now. They pretend not to know each other.

Once inside, Malothy tries to seem very grateful and friendly toward the PCs. "If you need a place to rest, or just some information," he says, "you should come see my friend Essatha." He then offers to show them how to get to her home. It might seem a little strange to observant or wary PCs that this rough-looking fellow is taking them up to where the high-class dwell, but they probably just arrived in the city and don't know its ways.

NYKA, AGAIN

Although the PCs probably met Nyka on the road, if they're not with the PCs when they reach Ketterach (assuming Nyka's still alive) and they haven't yet met with Essatha, the PCs "happen" to run into Nyka in the Crystal Shard. They put on all of their charm, pry into what the PCs are after, and eventually offer to take the PCs to meet a friend of theirs who can answer their questions or meet whatever needs they have. Nyka then takes them to Essatha's home.

IN HER HOME

Essatha greets her guests warmly, with fine wine and some delicious food. She welcomes the PCs and tries to put them at ease and find out more about them—she pretends that Nyka has not already told her all they know about the PCs.

What she really wants, besides trying to understand the PCs' goals and capabilities, is to get them to explore the Ancient Crèche or Hidden Stair and let her know what they find. In effect, she wants to make them allies (pawns, really, that she can betray later if need be).

She says that she has been to the Ancient Crèche (and she uses that term, which is likely the first time the PCs hear it), which is true. She's even willing to tell them how to get to what she considers the most interesting feature within, The Knowledge. If really pressed, or if she thinks it might win them over, she *might* give them the relevant information they can get from The Knowledge regarding the structure rising up from beneath Neandran. But this is a bargaining chip she won't use casually.

She's willing to tell them the following:

- It's called the Uldada.
- There is a component within it called the Abrustraithe. If connected to another device called the Dterrase, the Process building the structure can be stopped.
- The Dterrase lies within the Ancient Crèche, or a skilled crafter could build one of their own.

Ancient Crèche, page 61

Haunted Stair, page 50
Uldada, page 93
Crystal Shard, page 87

Nyka on the Trail, page 48

Malothy, page 108

The Ourach Invasion, page 100

The Knowledge, page 72

Abrustraithe, page 97

Essatha spins everything to get the PCs to go to the Ancient Crèche and bring whatever they find or learn back to her. So she can help them, of course. She's really just gathering all the intel she can. She'll even offer (honestly) that if they go there for her, she'll reward them with cyphers of their request when they return.

If they have already been to the Ancient Crèche and explored it thoroughly, she inquires as to what they found. This probably means that she has no long-term use for them, and when she's learned what she can from them, she suggests that it's time for them to leave.

If the PCs leave and they aren't going to work for Essatha, there are only two outcomes:

- The PCs are not worth considering anymore.
- The PCs are a threat, and thus must be killed.

It's also possible that the PCs might at some point try to break into Essatha's home. If they do, they can find out a great many things, but she will almost certainly find out. And the PCs will be marked for death.

Essatha's Home, page 88

MURDER

At no point will Essatha move against the PCs in her home, unless they attack her first. But if she's decided they need to be eliminated, she uses Nyka and Malothy to keep tabs on them, and when the PCs are in a vulnerable place, all three of them attack in concert. Essatha is ruthless, but she's not cruel. She just wants to get rid of any possible impediments. Her assistants, on the other hand, are bloodthirsty, and Malothy in particular delights in violence and pain.

Essatha is arrogant and assumes that she can handle any threat. If her life is seriously threatened, though, she attempts to flee. One can be certain, however, that she will try again, with a new strategy and a way to overcome the PCs' strengths. She is a formidable opponent.

WORKING WITH HER

As long as the PCs serve her purposes, she will happily supply them with crafted numenera and information (as long as it doesn't reveal anything about her plans). This is, after all, how she found herself with two loyal assistants. For a while, it might seem as if Essatha is a sort of patron for the PCs. She attempts to steer them away from any knowledge of the Naracodium, because she doesn't want the Uldada entirely undone. She also tries to keep them from obtaining the Dterrase, but she can live with it should she fail at that.

She has no loyalty, however, and no compassion. She will betray those working with her if doing so suits her.

ASSISTANTS

Essatha has two assistants that all but obey her every word, mostly out of gratitude for what she has given them.

NYKA

Nyka was an abandoned orphan living on the streets, cruelly rejected for their disabilities. Essatha exploited Nyka's needs by fitting them with mech parts. She's upgraded those parts again and again, all the while encouraging Nyka's activities as a pickpocket, a con artist, and a thief.

Nyka is quite short, and their cheeks each bear a thin synth plate enhancing their features in an artificial but not unattractive manner. Their left arm is made of metal and synth, and two of the fingers of her right hand are likewise artificial. The most dramatic enhancements they now possess, however, remain out of sight most of the time. Nyka has two additional arms, attached to artificial hips, but these arms exist out of phase with reality until Nyka wills it otherwise. In fact, they can even phase just a part of their arms into reality, allowing them to conjure just a thumb and forefinger inside a pocket they wish to pick. Nyka cannot alter the phase of objects other than their arms, so if they do pick a pocket in this way, the finger, thumb, and pilfered item must slip back to them conventionally, but they excel at doing so without being noticed.

Nyka carries a variety of knives hidden on their person, and a stingcharge holstered at their side. They also have a level 5 metal death cypher. Their armor is built into their body.

Naracodium, page 80

Nyka: *level 4; level 5 for Speed defense; level 6 for deception, stealth, and lock picking; level 7 for pickpocketing; Armor 2*

Stingcharge, page 98
Metal death cypher, page 283

CONVERSING WITH ESSATHA

In conversation with the PCs, Essatha doesn't have much interest in topics other than the Uldada, the Ancient Crèche, or the Haunted Stair. She is not overly concerned about the ourach invasion, has no interest in Ketterach politics or events, and can't be bothered with anything else regarding the valley or even the world beyond. If asked about her own past she says that she came here "a few years ago from a dull little place far away," and if asked about what she does, she "tinkers and studies the relics of the ancient past."

MALOTHY

Once a member of a very violent gang in Ketterach, Malothy is slight and just below average height. He wears his hair in a striking violet mohawk and his scarred face in a permanent sneer. His wiry limbs are muscular, and he conceals a wide variety of weapons all over his body.

Malothy's loyalty to Essatha comes from the two devices that she has crafted for him. The first is a potent invisible shield surrounding his body that he can quickly turn on and off with a bite-activated switch in his mouth. The second is a horrendous weapon he calls his skeever, which looks a bit like a spiked mace. The skeever has two different functions (beyond just being a nasty melee weapon). The first is that with the press of a button, the spikes detach and transform into hornet-like constructs that target all moving creatures in immediate range other than the wielder. The second is that it can create a cloud of thick, greasy smoke in an immediate area. Malothy uses this second function to escape if need be. The skeever is a level 6 artifact, with a depletion of 1 in 1d10, but it's always a nasty weapon.

In addition, Malothy carries a number of knives of different shapes and sizes, a forearm blade, and a buzzer. He has a single cypher in the form of a level 6 injector that restores 6 points of Speed.

THE PLAN

Not originally from the Glimmering Valley, Essatha arrived about two years ago, having learned of the dream, the Uldada,, and the ancient structure's imminent appearance. Further research and exploration allowed her to learn of The Knowledge in the Ancient Crèche. She went there and spoke with it directly (but explored very little of the rest of the complex).

She did not want to alert the Aeon Priests in Ketterach, whom she believed were already watching her activities with suspicion. She also wanted to keep them busy because she was certain they were also interested in the Ancient Crèche and the Uldada. (She is slightly paranoid—they are unaware of her, the Ancient Crèche, or the Uldada.) Thus, Essatha went to the region where the nearby ouarchs dwelt and used a telepathy cypher to implant the idea in their leader to come to the valley. Convinced that her enemies would be occupied with a full-on invasion, she proceeded to use one-use flying automaton drones to plant cameras at the entrance of the Ancient Crèche, at the site of the Uldada (Neandran), and just to be on the safe side, the Haunted Stair. She didn't know anything about the stair, but she suspected it was more than it seemed, unlike the River Ring or the Empty Caves, which turned up nothing of interest.

She believes that the completed Uldada will provide the means for her to tap into an extraterrestrial power source potent enough to give her everything she wants.

This means that the endgame for her comes at the very last stage of the Uldada's construction, when she shows up in person in Neandran. She has crafted a new artifact, one that she calls "The Door to the Future." She uses it to create a door in the side of the Uldada, and then passes through that door. She closes the door behind her and is very likely never seen on Earth again. Did she travel to another world? Another time? Another state of reality? No way to tell. But presumably, in so doing she amasses power, knowledge, or both.

This is why she considers anything that might permanently stop or reverse the Uldada, or anyone who might be interested in stopping her, as her greatest threats. Perhaps her only threats.

CHAPTER
13

CREATURES OF THE VALLEY

The following are full write-ups for some of the major creatures that live in the Glimmering Valley or make a prominent appearance in the events of the campaign.

BAROON 3 (9)

Small hunters

Baroon are a colony organism sharing traits of both insects and flightless birds. Their six legs and segmented bodies make them sturdy and strong, but a fourth pair of much longer extendable limbs allows them to run at great speeds in short bursts, or the limbs can be used as talons to defend themselves.

Baroon GM intrusion: *The angry baroon makes a sudden, additional attack with their beak (4 damage).*

Motive: Hunger for small game

Environment: The forests of the Glimmering Valley

Health: 9

Damage Inflicted: 3 points

Movement: Long; occasionally very long for one round

Modifications: Speed defense as level 5

Combat: Baroon use their speed to catch prey in their beak-like mouth. If attacked, they use their talons to defend. They usually flee from larger creatures, but if they are harmed they become intensely angry and attack with no thought for self-preservation.

Interaction: These animals are crafty, but not incredibly intelligent, and belligerently vengeful. Folks in the valley just leave them be. "Angrier than a baroon" is a saying in Neandran.

Use: Baroon offer a decent barometer of an area. If one sees a baroon in the woods, it means that there is (better) small game about, and probably no large predators.

BRIINII 3 (9)

Standoffish biomechanical humanoids

Briinii GM intrusion: *The briinii grabs one of the character's cyphers or artifacts and uses it against them.*

Briinii are biomechanical beings of great intellect but mysterious disposition. Long ago, these humanoids' ancestors built a civilization based on technology but discovered that it did not improve their existence. They turned away from this life and now live as nomads, their past civilization and even the rejection of it so far in the past that it is essentially forgotten. In their simple lives as hunters and gatherers, they avoid the numenera for the most part.

Ironically, briinii are well-suited to interacting with the devices that they traditionally eschew. Their biomechanical nature grants them the ability to interface with machines through fibers that extend from their flesh, and they can sense energy coursing through machines.

Motive: Safety

Environment: The Glimmering Valley in the winter; nomadic the rest of the year

Health: 9

Armor: 1 (2 against energy attacks)

Damage Inflicted: 3 points

Movement: Short

Modifications: Working with machines as level 4, stealth and hunting as level 4

Combat: Briinii use spears and long, slightly curved blades they call sesh. They wear leather armor of their own design studded with small bits of metal, and they are naturally resistant to energy attacks.

Interaction: Briinii are generally suspicious of other intelligent species.

Use: They are difficult friends to make, but as allies, briinii are stalwart and giving. And surprisingly good with technology.

Loot: Only commonplace items

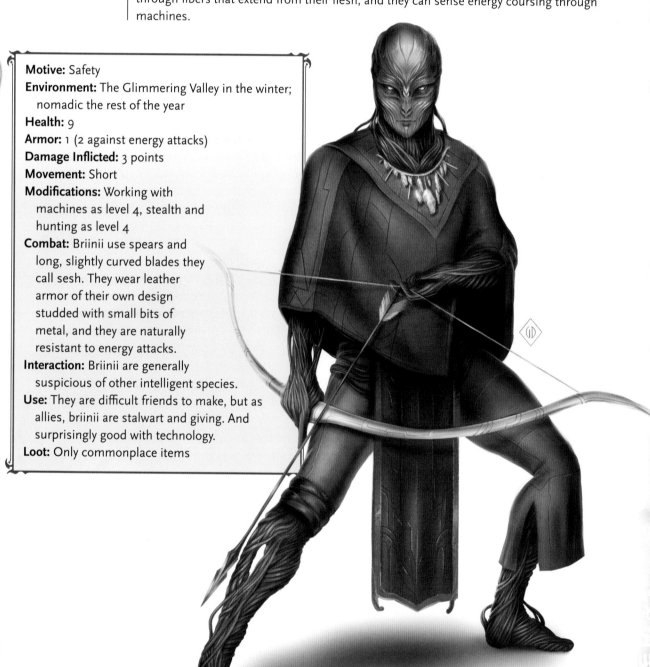

CHICHACHI 6 (18)

Mysterious glowing inchworms of incredible size

Named for the sound they seem to whisper, these creatures resemble enormous bioluminescent inchworms that make their way through the woods. No one has ever seen one eat, and no one has ever found a nest or lair. Shrouded in mystery, they may not be natives—or even residents—of this world.

Seeing a chichachi is rare and considered a good omen—killing one is thought to bring disaster upon all involved.

Motive: Safety

Environment: The Glimmering Valley

Health: 30

Armor: 1

Damage Inflicted: 6 points

Movement: Short

Modifications: Speed defense as level 3

Combat: Chichachi do not fight. If they inflict damage, it is through happenstance, such as if someone is in their way when they move or turn.

It's possible—perhaps even likely—that chichachi have the ability to fade in and out of existence, or slip into another universe. This would explain how something so large and literally glowing could remain unseen in the woods.

Interaction: It's possible that chichachi are quite intelligent, but no one has ever been able to communicate with one.

Use: Encountering a chichachi is a moment of quiet awe. Anyone that would violate such a thing—say, a band of wandering ouarchs—deserves to be shown the error of their ways.

Loot: Deep within the flesh of a chichachi lies a metallic heart that can be fairly easily converted into a random artifact.

Chichachi
GM intrusion: *The chichachi disappears and if the character fails an Intellect defense task, the chichachi takes them too.*

CORENDA 4 (12)

Attack hounds of the ourach

Corenda GM intrusion:
The corenda lashes a limb around the character, and the character must succeed at a Might-based task to get free.

One only sees a corenda in the service of ouarchs, and only when there are cormentals present. These vicious attack hounds have six-jointed limbs, making them seem more like tendrils than legs. A corenda uses these flexible limbs to cling to the underside of a cormental charging into battle (usually with an ourach on top), and then quickly detach to attack foes when commanded. They can do so even if the cormental charges at top speed, literally hitting the ground running, and launching an attack to one side or the other of the galloping beast.

Motive: Obey their ourach masters

Environment: Wherever the ourach go

Health: 12

Damage Inflicted: 4 points

Movement: Short

Combat: In their initial pouncing attack, the corenda makes two attacks against a single foe, each inflicting 4 points of damage. If both attacks hit, the victim must succeed at a Might defense roll or be knocked prone, with the corenda atop. While in this position, attacks the corenda makes are eased.

Interaction: Corenda are natural predators, trained and abused by ourach. They are unpleasant.

Use: Ourach use corenda as attack hounds in battle, and guardians of their camp when not in battle.

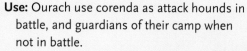

CORMENTAL 3 (9)

Mounts of the ourach and corenda

Swift, long-legged mounts, cormentals serve as steeds for their ourach masters. Probably descendants of some long-ago species of omnivore, cormentals have been bred to be strong, broad-bodied, and fearless. Their treatment at the hands of the ourach makes them angry and violent, but subservient to their masters.

Motive: Obey their ourach masters

Environment: Wherever the ourach go

Health: 10

Armor: 1

Damage Inflicted: 4 points

Movement: Short

Combat: Cormentals are not naturally armored, but the ourachs give them barding of leather and metal. As they charge into battle, they use their teeth to gore enemies.

Interaction: Temperamental, brutish, and mean-spirited, cormentals serve as mounts for ourach.

Use: Ourach use cormentals as mounts, and they are trained for combat.

Cormental
GM intrusion: *The cormental charges and not only attempts to gore the character, but tramples them if they can't get out of the way, inflicting 5 damage.*

The ourach, after making a successful attack against the character, wipes their blood on their avian face. The character must succeed at an Intellect defense roll or become hindered from fear while fighting the ourach.

OURACH   3 (9)

Merciless abhuman raiders

Like most abhumans, ourachs disdain most of the desirable aspects of humanity. They live to conquer, laying waste to an area and then moving on to the next.

Cruelty and violence are particularly honed concepts for the ourach. While they do not feed on fear, the smell of fear chemicals—and especially human fear chemicals—gives them great pleasure. It is both intoxicating and addicting for them. Their drive to terrorize others stands paramount to all other desires.

Motive: Conquest

Environment: Anywhere

Health: 9

Armor: 1

Damage Inflicted: 3 points

Movement: Short

Modifications: Attacks as level 4 when mounted, all actions as level 2 if confused or routed

Combat: The savage ourach craft armor and weapons from the bones of their victims. They use javelins at range, but in close quarters they use their natural claws and beak. They operate well in units, often accompanied by corenda, and riding cormentals.

Ourach commanders are level 5. They inflict 5 points of damage and, have 16 health and 2 Armor. If an ourach commander is killed, those they commanded usually immediately fall into disarray, although they do not automatically flee.

Interaction: Ourach speak the Truth, but do not read or write. They are bestial, cruel, selfish, and violent. The smell of fear gives them pleasure.

Use: Ourach are terrifying opponents, but one with a weakness (their inability to even comprehend contingencies). Once that weakness is discovered, the ourach can be defeated.

Loot: Ourach commanders usually have a cypher or even an artifact.

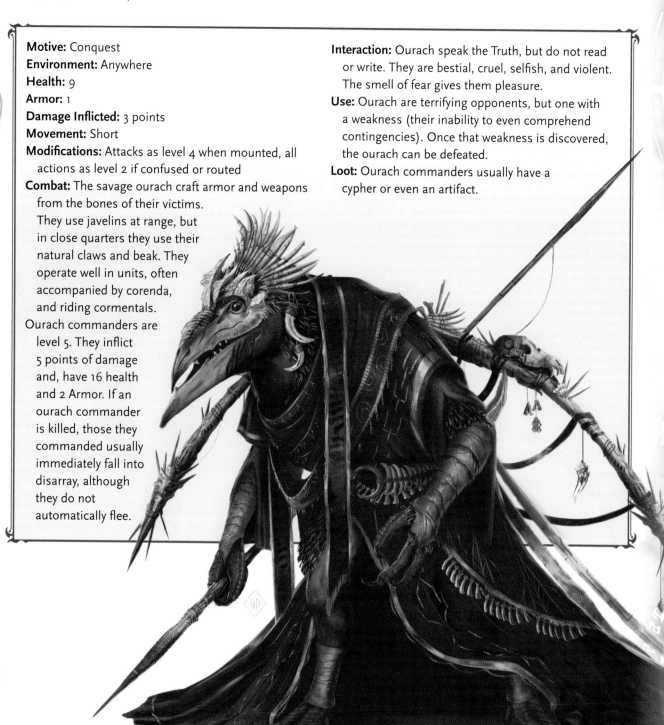

REAN 3 (9)

Fast, observant herbivores

These graceful bipedal herbivores are known for their extreme wariness and heightened senses. Only the most skilled hunter can bring down a rean, but those that can are rewarded with a lot of highly prized meat.

Motive: Safety

Environment: The woods of the Glimmering Valley

Health: 9

Armor: 2

Damage Inflicted: 3 points

Movement: Long, with one-round bursts of very long

Modifications: All Speed defense, perception tasks, jumping, and climbing as level 6

Combat: Rean use their small horns to attack, but only when it's impossible to flee.

Interaction: Rean have the typical intelligence of an animal.

Use: Hunting a rean and bringing back the meat is a rite of passage for any hunter in the valley.

Rean GM intrusion: *The rean inadvertently hooks their antlers on the character's pack, belt, or some other likely object, tearing it away and running off with great speed.*

SARRAT

5 (15)

Large chemical-spewing cats

These large feline predators have glands that can spit hallucinogenic chemicals to confuse prey and make them easier to bring down. Sarrata (the plural of sarrat) do not hesitate to attack humans or even larger prey, often operating in mated trios. They lair in caves along the valley walls, raising a litter of three to five young every spring, or every other spring.

The similarity in name as well as general physiognomy to the sarrak involves no coincidence. They are (very) distantly related creatures.

Sarrak, page 250

Sarrat GM intrusion: *The hallucinations linger for the character, recurring every hour or so until they get a full night's sleep or some kind of antidote. Atta (page 39) offers the antidote as one of her elixirs.*

Motive: Hunger for flesh

Environment: The woods of the Glimmering Valley, often in trios

Health: 15

Armor: 1

Damage Inflicted: 5 points

Movement: Short

Modifications: Jumping and climbing as level 6

Combat: Sarrata begin their attack by spitting chemicals up to an immediate distance, targeting one foe or two adjacent foes. Without a successful Might defense task, the victim experiences hallucinations for the next three rounds. On the first round, the victim can take no action (even defensive actions) as they are utterly unaware of their surroundings. On the second round, they can perceive true reality a bit, but all actions (including defensive actions) are hindered by 2 steps. On the third and final round, they are still experiencing mild hallucinations and are hindered in all actions by 1 step. Once they have affected an opponent with their chemicals, the sarrat pounces and attacks the bewildered target with teeth and claws.

Interaction: Sarrata are much more intelligent than simple animals, but they do not have a language.

Use: From time to time, a sarrat begins to prey on the gobrin around Neandran and will not stop until the villagers hunt them down.

Loot: Sarrat saliva is a hallucinogen. Using it is very much frowned on in Neandran, but trading it to visiting merchants for the equivalent of 12 shins? That's just good business.

TOOTHED EYE 6 (18)

Prior-world biomechanical entity with strange powers

The toothed eye is a prior-world fusion of bio-engineering and mechanical design. It is tied somehow to the Uldada, and at some point in the Process of that structure's development it emerges from its buried lair (more of a suspended animation chamber, really) and searches for the Uldada. Why doesn't it already know where the structure is? No one knows. After a few weeks of searching the valley, though, it finds the Uldada and takes up a position guarding it.

The eye floats through the air about 6 feet (2 m) from the ground. It can rotate quickly and seems to always be scanning about, taking in all of its surroundings. In a very real way, the creature is a floating maw with a huge eye inside of it, clearly visible when the mouth is open (which is all of the time, unless it's biting something).

Uldada, page 93

The Lair of the Toothed Eye, page 43

Motive: Find and protect the Uldada
Environment: The woods of the Glimmering Valley
Health: 24
Armor: 3
Damage Inflicted: 6 points
Movement: Long
Modifications: Perception as level 8, Might and Intellect defense as level 7
Combat: The toothed eye projects deadly heat rays at a target within very long range that it can see. A victim suffers 4 points of heat damage, plus they must succeed at a Might defense roll or spend the next round on the ground on fire, putting out the flames, suffering an additional 4 points of damage. In melee, it bites with its terrible synth teeth.

Interaction: Communication, let alone reasoning, with the toothed eye is impossible. It seems to be moderately intelligent, but more like a trained animal than a person.
Use: The toothed eye can be encountered in the woods searching, where it will ignore anyone that doesn't attack it, or at the site of the Uldada, where it protects the Uldada from intrusion.
Loot: If destroyed, the remains of the toothed eye hold the components for three random cyphers.

Toothed eye
GM intrusion: *The toothed eye projects a powerful heat ray at the ground beneath a character's feet, melting the ground. This not only potentially harms the character as a normal heat ray attack, but on the following round they are stuck in the re-solidifying ground.*

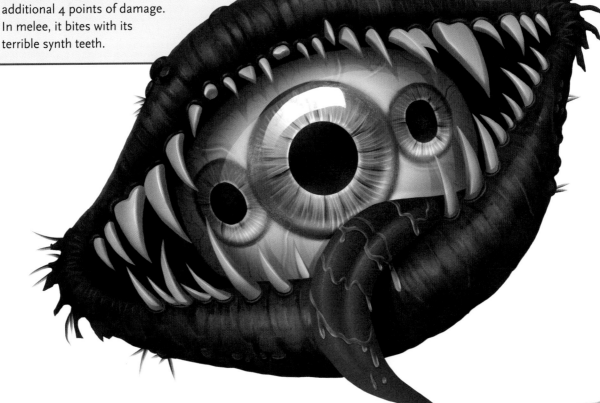

Tyr-ana GM intrusion:
Although the branches aren't prehensile, a rash move by the tyr-ana causes them to brush against the character and everyone else in the immediate area, subjecting them all to not only an attack but the branches' poison as well.

TYR-ANA

4 (12)

Intelligent, carnivorous trees that walk

These extremely rare trees have crimson, leafless branches. Most notably, however, their lower trunks appear to have two humanoid legs and they can uproot themselves and walk. Carnivorous, they feed on small mammals and birds they lure into their scented branches, covered in poisonous barbs. Tyr-ana can only move their legs, not their branches.

Motive: Hunger for flesh

Environment: The woods of the Glimmering Valley

Health: 15

Armor: 3

Damage Inflicted: 4 points

Movement: Short

Modifications: Perception as level 3; running, jumping, swimming, or climbing as level 1

Combat: Tyr-ana emit pleasant scents, and any creature within immediate distance must succeed at a Might defense task to avoid the compulsion to get up into the tree's branches. The branches have poisonous barbs that inflict 4 points of Speed damage (ignores Armor) to anyone that fails a Might defense task. Against a threat that does not succumb to the compulsion, the tyr-ana lashes out with their only animate part—their "legs."

Interaction: Tyr-ana do not typically hunt prey as large as a human, but they will fight if they must. They do not react to attempts at communication or even seem aware of the concept.

Use: Tyr-ana are almost otherworldly in appearance and manner. GMs should use them to unnerve players as much as to challenge PCs.

Loot: The sap of the tyr-ana is a potent but temporary stimulant. This operates exactly like a stim cypher. Each tree has enough sap for 1d6 + 2 such cyphers.

Stim cypher, page 287

VEESHIN 2 (6)

Snakes that hunt in packs

Veeshin are snakes that have evolved into a pack hunting predator. They operate in a pack of no fewer than eight and sometimes as many as two dozen at a time. Unlike many other serpents, they do not swallow prey whole. Instead, they secrete acid that breaks down the flesh of their prey so that they can easily swallow the almost-liquified remains. They're known for their brilliant colors and their hissing, which many liken to a "sizzling" sound.

Motive: Hunger for flesh

Environment: The Glimmering Valley and throughout the surrounding mountains

Health: 6

Armor: 1

Damage Inflicted: 2 points

Movement: Short

Modifications: Speed defense as level 4

Combat: Veeshin venom inflicts an additional 2 points of Speed damage against anyone bitten who fails a Might defense task. When operating as a pack/swarm, four of the serpents attack as a single level 4 creature, inflicting 4 points of damage, and their poison inflicts 4 points of Speed damage. If there are four of these small packs, they can all operate as a single level 6 creature, inflicting 6 points of damage with a poison that inflicts 6 points of Speed damage.

Interaction: Veeshin are simply animals.

Use: Veeshin are the terrors of the valley that folks generally fear most. A nest of them in a cave or a fallen tree anywhere near the village, if discovered, presents a threat to both residents and gobrin (and other animals the residents hunt). The village sends out a team of armed folk—usually just before sunrise, when the snakes are least active—to kill them or drive them off. Atta keeps a supply of veeshin antivenin that restores points of Speed lost and prevents further Speed drain for a few hours after the application.

Veeshin GM intrusion: *The pack attacks the character and slithers up their pant leg or into their cloak. Not only are the snakes' attacks eased, but attacking them is difficult without harming the victim.*

Atta, page 39

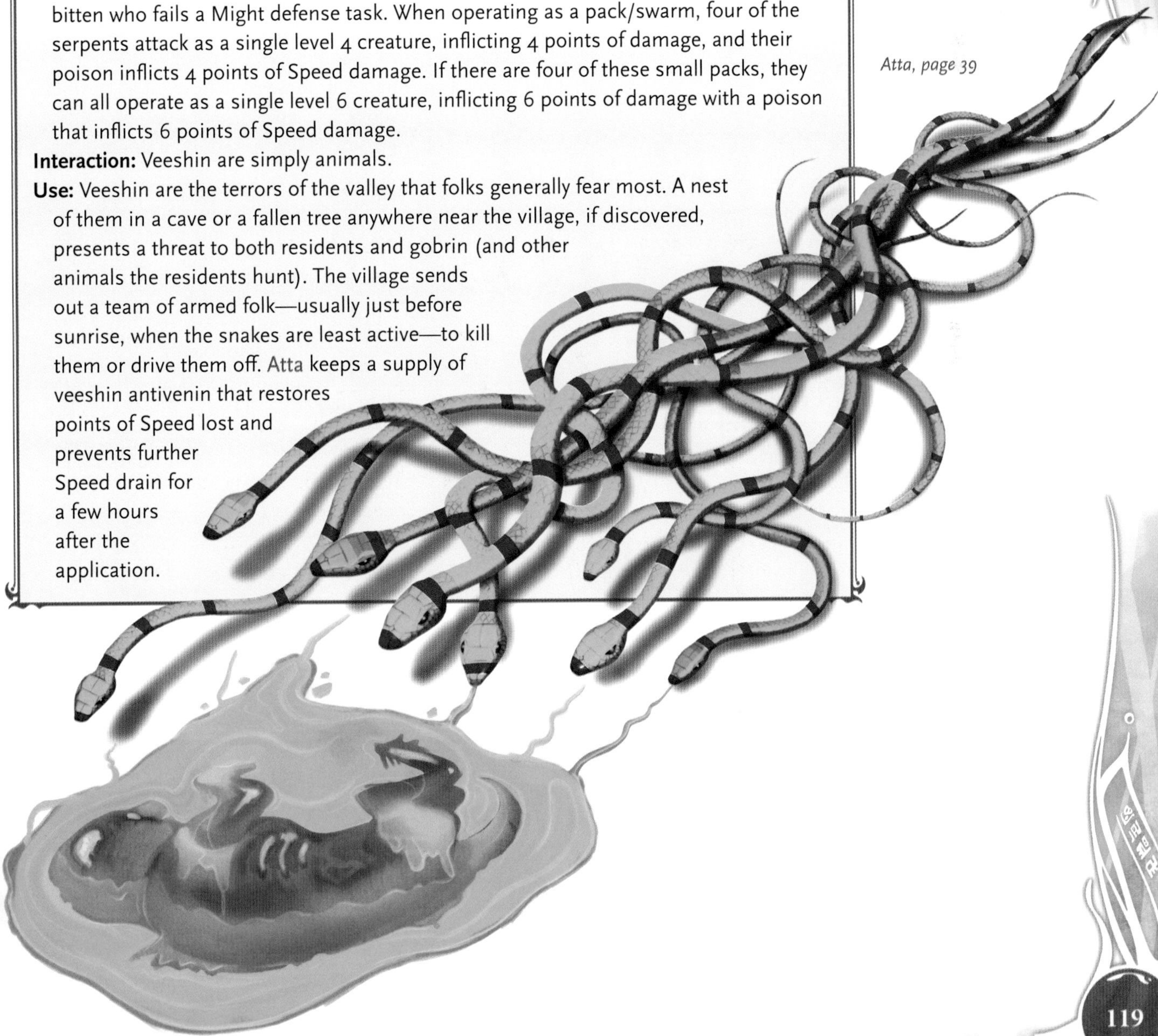

CHAPTER
14

THE PLAYER'S GUIDE

How blessed, how very blessed we are to call a place like Neandran home. It's a cold, dangerous world that shows no mercy to the gentle, the careful, or the wise, let alone the young, the weak, or the brash. But safely enclosed by the arms of Neandran, deep within the hidden crags and lush forests of the Glimmering Valley, we are cared for, protected, and nurtured as well as any could hope in this world.

You look around and know that the world is very old. Even the valley itself was shaped by people who lived long ago. You can see their handiwork here and there in the valley's walls, in some of the nearby empty ruins, or in the temple at the very heart of Neandran. There are those in the village that believe the ancient creators of such things were not people, but rather demons of ancient days. The loudest voice behind such thoughts is Easchel, but we'll get to the specifics of the village's colorful folk soon enough.

THE DREAM

Everyone in Neandran has the same dream each night, without exception. It's the only dream we've ever known (and in fact the very concept that someone might have a different dream is unknown to us). Some people even occasionally experience the dream as a waking vision as well as when sleeping. It's always there, and in a way it ties us all together.

Now, I cannot truthfully tell you what the dream is, or what it is about, or even describe it to an outsider. I don't have the words to do so and they don't have the words to understand me if I did.

The dream swims with images, shapes, and even colors you won't see anywhere else. Over the years, folk have come up with names for some of them. There's the color *vell*, a creature they call the toothed eye, a structure named the growing forest of steel, and a sound called the wailing of the wood. But these names don't really help to explain or understand.

The important thing to know is that we have always had the dream. And less than two weeks ago, it began to change. The images shifted. There were new sights and sounds, but all just as inexplicable as before. Everyone's talking about it but no one has any explanations.

NEANDRAN

Thates Fields

To Lake Memory
Gobrin Grazing
To The River Dock
To The Mill

2 13

12

1

Crystal Monolith

Storehouse

10

Crystal Monolith

Temple

5

11

6

4

Thates Fields

7

9

1. Aryle and Amrose's House
2. Easchel's House
3. Gonnor's House
4. Illace's House
5. Sesson and Ien's House
6. Kyath and Ulam's House
7. Luttan's House
8. Mert's House
9. Messos and Thear's House
10. Rystan's House
11. Odet's House
12. Verge's House
13. Veri and Yurran's House

Storehouses

The Post

3

8

250 feet
76 meters

To the Infinite Abode

THE VILLAGE

You've lived in Neandran your whole life. There's no one among its four hundred and some inhabitants that you haven't met and likely spoken to many times. Likewise, we all know you. We remember that foolish thing you did when you were younger, but also the achievements you've accomplished as well. We know your family, and we know your friends. We are your family and friends.

While technically the folk of the village utilize a barter system, the truth is Luttan makes sure that everyone has what they need when they need it. Shins are used only to deal with the occasional trader that comes to the village from far-off Ketterach, bringing things the village doesn't provide on its own, like metal, sugar, spices, and more. Concepts like individualized wealth or social class have no meaning in Neandran.

SOME FOLK OF THE VILLAGE

Among all the residents, listed here are some that are the most prominent, or at least the most memorable.

Although there is no leader of the village, everyone more or less defers to Amrose, not because she asks for such a thing, but because she deserves it with her wisdom and foresight.

Alloise is a leatherworker that is married to Gonnor.

Aryle, partner of Amrose, is a beloved and entertaining fellow. Since you were young, you've seen him perform tricks, tell stories, and do all sorts of endearing things—with a focus on the village's children, but most adults find him entertaining as well. He's always quick to help out when and where he's needed for regular work as well. A good fellow, to be sure.

Bik (short for Bichel) is a broad-faced, shiny-cheeked man who maintains the Post, where many folks in the village gather in the evening to relax, eat, drink, and talk.

Amrose

Aryle

Easchel is an advocate for the old ways. By that, he means that simple village life is superior to that of any city, and that anything that smacks of sorcery should be avoided at all costs. That means any strange abilities, ancient devices, and so on.

Gonnor is a craftsman who works with stone and metal. He seems sad a lot of the time, so try to be nice. That is, if you can find him.

Ien is a fisherman and is married to Sesson. He seems to have recurring stomach pains recently, and visits Verge the healer quite frequently.

Illace cooks and takes in sewing and mending. She is elderly and generally helpful and friendly.

Despite the physical mutations he's had since birth, **Jofan** works odd jobs throughout the village and is a very capable handyman.

Kyath works as a farmer but used to be a warrior from Ketterach. If you know anything about combat, it's probably thanks to Kyath's instruction, although he now spends most of his time farming.

Luttan manages the village storehouses. She ensures everyone has what they need. There isn't a "store" or a "market" in Neandran, but if you need something, just track down Luttan.

Mert is a hunter and tracker and knows the woods of the valley better than anyone. She's not around much, but when she is, she's often at the Post, drinking.

Messos is a woodsman. He is married to Thear, and father to their children.

Narth works with Messos, and the two of them cut and prepare wood for the village.

Odet oversees the mill. Despite her age, she's handy with her fists, and if you know anything about unarmed fighting, it might be thanks to her.

Rystan is a glassblower and a bit of a gossip.

Easchel

Gonnor

Kyath

Odet

Illace

Luttan

Rystan

Jofan

Mert

Sesson is a priest of Loe and he performs rituals in the temple. Loe is a nurturing and loving god that helps those in need, if they truly deserve it (at least, that's what the teachings say). Sesson is married to Ien.

Thear is a highly skilled woodworker. She's married to Messos and they have two children.

Udya is Kyath's partner, and she cares for their three children.

Ulam is an aged widow that lives alone.

Verge is a healer with a gruff demeanor.

Veri works as a baker with her husband Yurran. She is the adult daughter of Aryle and Amrose.

Yurran is Veri's husband and is also a baker.

Sesson

Thear

Verge

PLACES IN THE VILLAGE

At the very center of Neandran stands the temple. It's an ancient structure, and some claim it wasn't even built by human hands. Sesson, the village priest, holds rites and ceremonies in honor of Loe.

If you're looking for someone once the workday is done, the Post is likely where you should start your search. It's a gathering place where all are welcome, and a friendly fellow named Bik serves food and drink for all that wish it.

The crystal monoliths stand equidistant from the Temple, and seem likely to be just as old. Everyone knows that they give off some kind of energy or influence and cause strange things to happen. Children born in the village sometimes possess physical mutations, while a few others have abilities that most folk here call sorcery. And that's a bit frightening. Still, the wisest of us also know that this same essence makes our farmland so fertile and our flocks so healthy.

The village has multiple storehouses of food and supplies.. Luttan is in charge of all of them and she keeps a careful tally of all the village's stores.

While Neandran boasts woodcutters, hunters, fisherfolk, and many other roles, none are as important or as numerous as the farmers and herders. Folks work long hours in the fields growing thates. These tubers can be cooked in any of a number of ways, or even ground to make flour for bread. Other folks tend to the flocks of gobrin—shaggy grey goat-like creatures—that supply us milk, wool, and sometimes meat.. Don't be surprised if you see one with more legs than it should have, or even two heads. That's just the way we grow them here in the valley.

Some of the villagers' pet seskii help with the gobrin herds, but not all.

Many sacks of thates are toted down to the river where they're ground into flour in the mill, upriver from the fishing-boat docks.

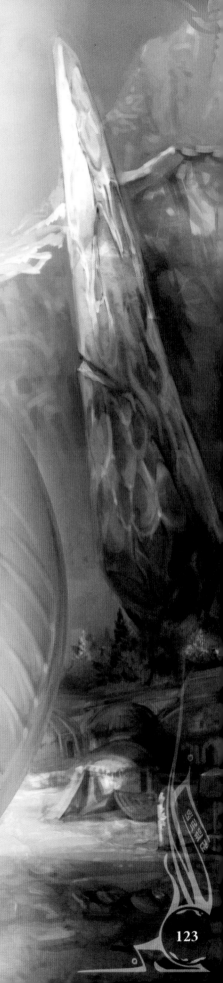

AVAILABLE STARTING CHARACTER OPTIONS

Not all of the character options found in *Discovery* and *Destiny* are available for characters starting in Neandran.

DESCRIPTOR

You can take any descriptor you want except for Cultured. You're human. The visitants presented in the rules are unknown in Neandran.

TYPE

You can choose to play a Glaive, a Nano, or a Jack. No one in Neandran has ever heard of an Arkus, a Wright, or a Delve. The GM will have more information if you desire.

FOCUS

The GM might have additional notes or thoughts regarding a character's focus. You can choose from any of the following foci:

Acts Without Consequence
Controls Beasts
Defends the Gate
Defends the Weak
Entertains
Explores Dark Places
Explores Yesterday
Fights With Panache
Hunts
Imparts Wisdom
Leads
Learns From Adversity
Lives in the Wilderness
Masters Defense
Masters Weaponry
Moves Like a Cat
Needs No Weapons
Never Says Die
Rages
Shepherds the Community
Speaks With a Silver Tongue
Talks to Machines
Wields Two Weapons at Once
Wields Words Like Weapons

You can also choose from the foci listed below, wielding powers probably resulting from a life spent in the energies of the crystal monoliths. However, keep in mind that folk in the village are cautious of overt "strange powers" and some are quite hostile to the appearance of such "sorcery," so there can be difficulties associated with these foci. You'll likely have to determine how you have been trying to conceal your abilities, especially from Easchel.

Absorbs Energy
Bears a Halo of Fire
Brandishes an Exotic Shield
Breaks Down Walls
Commands Mental Powers
Controls Gravity
Crafts Illusions
Emerged From the Obelisk
Employs Magnetism
Exists Partially Out of Phase
Focuses Mind Over Matter
Radiates Vitality
Rides the Lightning
Sees Beyond
Shreds the Walls of the World
Thunders
Touches the Sky
Wears a Sheen of Ice
Works Miracles

NAMES

People of Neandran don't use surnames. A single, typically one- or two-syllable name is most common, usually with moderately soft sounds like Amrose or Luttan. The only person with a hard K in their name is Kyath, and he's not originally from the village. Names usually end in a consonant sound.

Names are not tied to a gender or status.

Names usually cycle through the generations in a family, but never while the original name holder is alive. So Thear had a grandfather named Thear, and her parents named her because he had already passed by the time she was born. Her family won't name a child Thear again until she has, in turn, passed. Reusing the name of an ancestor is always meant to be a way of honoring the past.

While you can choose any single name you wish, try to make it fit with the others in the village.

FAMILIES AND FRIENDS

All PCs have family and friends in Neandran. Working with the GM, you should choose at least one and perhaps as many as five or six NPCs in the village. The PC is either related to or particularly friendly with these characters, perhaps even living in the same house as they do.

The village's population far exceeds the named NPCs, however, so there is ample room for new characters to be added as needed. For example, a character might know Veri and Yurran as they grew up right next door, and thus by extension they might know Amrose and Aryle (Veri's parents) fairly well, but your character's actual parents are NPCs of your creation.

Family and friends offer a way to explain the equipment and cyphers you start with, and perhaps the training you have in your skills and abilities. Encourage both comparing and contrasting NPCs with the PCs. That is to say, a PC who is friends with Luttan might be very well organized, smart, and devoted to the village, but they might also be friends with Mert, a skilled hunter and tracker, and also a bit of a troublemaker in town. Our friends sometimes complement our outlook, but they sometimes also provide interesting foils. Imagine the awkward situation where a PC who Bears a Halo of Fire lives next door to Easchel. Or perhaps Easchel is their father!

VILLAGE CONNECTIONS

Above and beyond knowing who their friends and family in Neandran might be, each PC should have a special link to one of the named NPCs. Pick a person in the village to have this strong connection to your character. Provide a narrative reason for the connection that ties in with your character's background.

Once per day (once between ten-hour rests), you can make the equivalent of a player intrusion but with no XP cost. However, the intrusion must relate to the connected NPC from the village.

For example:

- [Connected NPC] has the tool I need and happens to walk by so I can ask them for it.
- [Connected NPC] knows the cure for this malady and will share it with me.
- [Connected NPC] will hide us for the evening in their house.

The connection, of course, has the most value when players are in the village. In the valley outside the village, the connection can be called upon in less direct ways. Such intrusions might be linked to advice, gifts, or tiny bits of knowledge that happen to be useful in a given situation. Examples:

- [Connected NPC] told me about a plant that grows in deep gullies that might treat this poison.
- [Connected NPC] once mentioned these beasts and that they have an aversion to water.
- [Connected NPC] gave me this tool we need before we left the village.
- [Connected NPC] once showed me a trick to fix a broken bow like this.

Obviously, the intrusion has to fit the NPC as well as the situation. Ien could have shared insight about the best place to ford the river, but Easchel, who has never left Neandran, couldn't. Likewise, Alloise is unlikely to have had a rock-crafting tool to give the PC, but she might have given them something more suited to leatherworking.

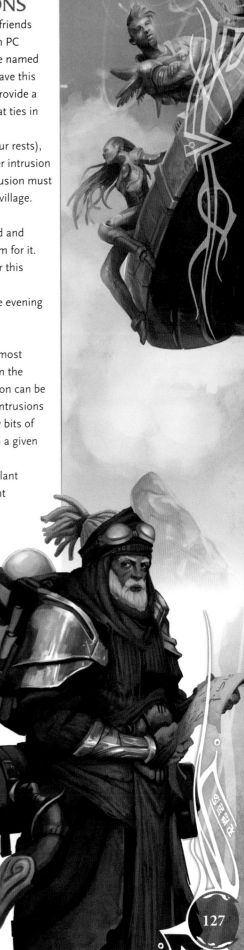

GLOSSARY AND INDEX

This is a list of all the major NPCs, creatures, places, devices, and concepts in the Glimmering Valley, and where you can find more information on each.